# Machine Embroidery

## Technique and Design

Jennifer Gray

**VNR** VAN NOSTRAND REINHOLD COMPANY

NEW YORK CINCINNATI TORONTO LONDON MELBOURNE

Van Nostrand Reinhold Company Regional Offices:
New York   Cincinnati   Chicago   Millbrae   Dallas

Van Nostrand Reinhold Company International Offices:
London   Toronto   Melbourne

Printed in Great Britain

Published by Van Nostrand Reinhold Company
A Division of Litton Educational Publishing Inc
450 West 33rd Street, New York, NY 10001

# Contents

# 1 Domestic and trade machines

The image of machine embroidery has changed considerably over the last ten years. This is due to a number of inter-related factors which have combined to increase interest and enable many more people to enjoy doing as well as seeing machine embroidery. One of the contributing factors is the advancement in recent years of sewing machine technology, particularly in the embroidery field. After buying a machine many people have been stimulated by its acquisition to develop the design and technique of embroidery by going to a centre for tuition.

There have also been, over the last ten years, many more books dealing with this particular subject which have encouraged fresh and individual ideas. Another great contributing factor towards its recognition as a form in its own right rather than an imitation of hand methods, is the large number of exhibitions organised by various individuals, educational bodies and groups who have made work available to the general public through exhibitions in galleries and libraries.

There was a period when embroidery could have developed into the mere exploitation of the machine to achieve precise technique alone. What has actually happened is far more exciting in that the capabilities of the machine have been harnessed in order to express ideas with life and sensitivity. The general climate of opinion towards machine embroidery is more sympathetic in the 1970s than it has ever been. This is no doubt due to the creative attitude taken by embroiderers in this field.

The primary production of the machine is texture, since a single stitch is set in relief to the ground, and even this is curved in coming up and going down through the fabric so that a change of tone is produced as the light falls on it displaying the sheen of the thread. The complexity of this is increased with its relation to the fabric which has a tremendous influence on the shape of the stitch depending on the quality of the weave. On organdie the machine embroidery thread being thicker than the woven yarn will give a crisp line whereas on hessian it will merge into the fabric tending to be lost in the weave because it is finer. This, coupled with the curving of the stitch, produces a greater contrast of tone from the thread, giving a speckled appearance to the line. The type of line can vary on the same fabric by an alteration of the tension, a completely straight one is possible where the upper thread is whipped by the lower and is not pulled down through the fabric. When the thread is pulled through a moderate to coarse weave the stitch is sometimes twisted slightly when the needle does not go cleanly through the woven threads but slides down between them. On relatively fine fabrics when the top tension is even or looser than the bottom, the stitch is slightly slanted because of the twisting of the upper thread with the lower. This varying in the angle of the stitch gives a sensitive characteristic to the line.

The different qualities of line achieved by different machines is worth considering. Both straight stitch and swing-needle domestic sewing machines can be used for automatic and free embroidery. The relative merits of modern machines vary slightly, the *Bernina* being perhaps the most trouble free, the *Viking* light and sensitive, the *Necchi* a good plodder as is the *Elna*. *Singers* vary considerably, some being heavy in action others more sensitive though given to breaking the cotton in free work. Satin stitch produced by these swing-needle machines is an important feature of machine embroidery. The fully-automatic machines with built-in cams to produce repetitive patterns are of less use for free embroidery than the cheaper semi-automatics. Both can be used for plain sewing as well as buttonholes and over-casting, and the semi-automatic can be used for a certain amount of automatic decoration. They are generally fairly robust and will stand a good deal of changing from sewing to embroidery without trouble.

Trade machines are designed primarily for free embroidery and possess rather more complex characteristics than the domestic machines, being designed for specific types of embroidery.

The semi-automatic swing-needle machines mentioned in this chapter are those with which I have been most familiar over the last ten years and it is with their particular qualities that this chapter is most concerned. Other and more recent machines have similar as well as different qualities but it would be unwieldy to deal with them all. Most of them cope in different ways with the same problem made necessary by the use of the machine for embroidery as well as sewing. The realisation of these problems has been very well met by continental engineers and has resulted in the stream-lining of the design of modern machines.

# Domestic machines

The *Necchi Lycia* (working from left to right) has a broad table extension sometimes a little difficult to attach. The door in the base of the machine swings open for the insertion of the spool case from the left. It is unnecessary to remove the extension table in order to do this. The top threading is rather more complex than other domestic machines and takes a fraction longer. The needle is threaded from the left and the range from loose to tight tension is wide. The lever bringing into action the needle-throw-bar is adequate though a little narrow to hold when a good deal of shaped satin stitch is being worked. A switch in the base of the machine is twisted to drop the feed teeth. The winding of the bobbin is brought into operation when the door near the wheel at the front of the machine is opened and, because of two holders for cotton reels at the back of the machine when the twin needle is not in use, thread can be wound onto a spool whilst work is in progress. The power foot is brought into operation when the knob in the centre at the front is depressed. The foot being light in construction tends to wander despite rubber feet and the knob is therefore sometimes difficult to locate.

This is a hardworking machine, capable of accepting a number of different machinists without causing trouble, keeps in time well and is, on the whole, trouble free as far as breaking of thread is concerned.

*Necchi Lycia*

**Viking Husqvarna**   The *Viking Husqvarna* has an easily attached table extension which is narrower than the *Necchi* and does not have to be removed to insert the spool case in the front of machine base. The top threading is very quick and easy, the needle threading from the front. The range of the top tension is good. The swing-needle lever is large and easy to manipulate and despite the fact that it widens the throw of the needle-throw-bar when it is operated from right to left, contrary to other domestic machines, the worker is not particularly inconvenienced by this. The feed teeth are lowered by a knob being turned at the front of the machine. The spool is wound on a spindle on the right hand end of the machine beneath the wheel which brings a gear into operation, disconnecting the needle bar so that work can remain under the needle without being damaged while the spool is filling. The power foot is foot-like in shape and slightly angled so that when the whole of it is depressed, power is brought into operation fairly gradually so that some variation in the speed at which the machine runs is possible.

This is a sensitive machine producing quite a variety of work of a delicate nature. It is less given to the breaking of the top thread if it has one owner.

The *Bernina* semi-automatic machine is similar to the *Viking* in many ways, the table extension which is easy to attach is about the same width, the spool case loads at the front, the top threading is quick and easy and the needle threads from the front. The tension which is built inside the top of the machine is operated by a knurled wheel set towards the back of the machine and operates the plus and minus sign which indicates the type of tension being employed. The range of this is rather narrow and increases and decreases tension sharply towards both ends of its travel. The feed teeth are easily lowered by a knob which points either to stitching or darning. The spool is threaded by being placed on a spindle on the front of the machine which pushes it against the drive wheel. Machining can continue during winding but the rate of the needle is slowed down. The power foot is large and operates like the *Viking* allowing some regulation in the speed of the machine.

This machine of all the semi-automatics, seems to be the most trouble-free. Normal maintenance, that is regular oiling and removal of fluff and dust, is enough to keep the machine running without the need of a yearly overhaul. Its best feature is the snag-free mechanism which holds the spool case and prevents jamming produced by loose threads in the mechanism. The other advantage is that the cotton rarely breaks whilst stitching.

# Trade machines

*Viking Husqvarna*
The *Viking Husqvarna* trade machine is larger and more sturdily built than the domestic models. There is greater space between the needle and the vertical arm so that larger frames can be used to stretch the work and since the machine is set into a stand the whole table top is larger. The particular machine can be used for sewing as well as embroidery. The satin stitch throw is over 6 mm ($\frac{1}{4}$ in.) which is wider than most domestic machines can produce. The needle-throw-bar is brought into operation either by a hand operated lever or a knee press which leaves both hands free for the frame. The spool is wound against the drive-wheel, the feed teeth can be depressed and the large foot plate enables the machine to be run slowly when this is necessary. The complex top tension plates enables one to obtain very fine degrees of tension.

This is a hard working, dual sewing and embroidery machine almost touching the high quality of the trade embroidery machines but perhaps because it is not completely geared to embroidery it does after a time require expert attention if it is used for both sewing and embroidery.

*Irish machine*  The *Singer* swing-needle machine 107G102 has never been anything but an embroidery machine and benefits from that fact. All the parts which are not necessary for the production of embroidery have been removed, for instance the presser foot lever which brought the top tension into correct adjustment when it was lowered, has in the recent models been removed so that the correct tension for stitching has been built into the machine. The top tension screw is still at the front of the machine for the precise adjustment of the stitch. The threading of this machine is more complex but will speed up with practice. The spool case fits in from the back of the machine which sounds as though it would be awkward but once the knack is achieved is done very easily by feel, holding onto the latch to prevent the spool falling out, the hand is moved under the bed of the machine towards the back and then brought forward onto the spindle. The needle threads from the front. The spool is wound by pressing a wheel on the base of the machine against the leather belt so that spools can be filled whilst work is in progress. A knee press operates the needle-throw-bar which can produce a satin stitch throw of 12 mm ($\frac{1}{2}$ in.). The foot pedal is large and since the motor is geared can produce variable speeds from slow, as for cut-work, up to 1000 stitches a minute.

The great advantage of this swing-needle machine over domestic machines is the use of the knee press as this makes it possible to change from fine line to satin stitch without pause enabling a rhythm to be retained which adds to the sensitive quality of the work. No instructions for threading and setting up could be better than the machine's manual which explains not only tensions for straight and satin stitch but the adjustment of the machine for cording and Madeira (eyelet) embroidery.

16

**Cornelli and chain-stitch machines** Chain stitch is provided by the trade machines known as the *Cornelli* and *Singer* chain-stitch machines. Their performance is to some extent more limited than the *Irish*. They are able to vary the length of the stitch and the width of the line according to the size of plate and weight of thread used and can produce two versions of chain stitch as well as cording.

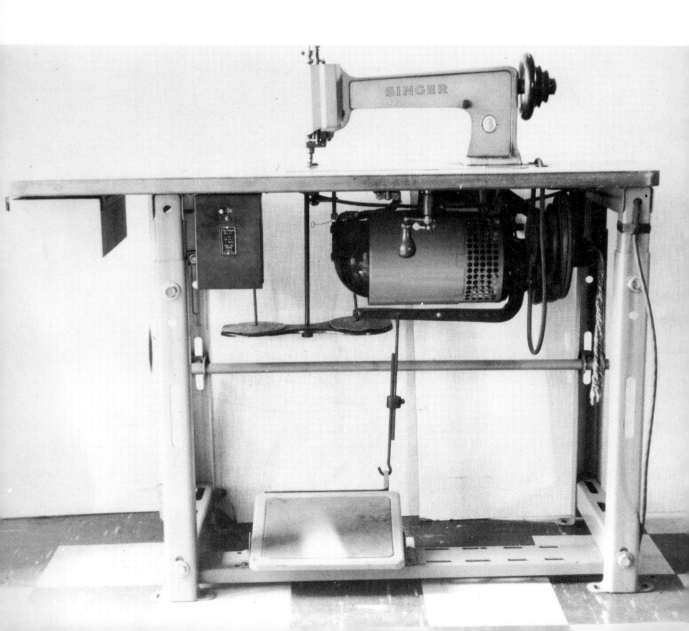

The one thread which forms the stitch must be suitable for both the hole in the cover plate and the hook of the needle, so that when it is brought up from beneath the plate it does not touch the sides of the hole. The fabric which is not placed in a frame is held down to the plate by a round foot, which moves the cloth for each stitch and, since it is connected with the guiding handle under the bed of the machine, also alters the direction in which it moves the fabric when this handle is brought into action. Since the handle of the machine works on the circle, curves and spirals can be produced as naturally as straight lines. The chain stitch formed gives a pleasant texture against straight and satin stitch and can be used in conjunction with these or entirely on its own, when variations in the thickness and type of thread as well as length of stitch can give variety with corded stitches, to the line. Moss stitch, detached chain stitch which forms a loop on the surface, is worked on the same principle as seeding, gives different textures depending on the type of threads used and the closeness with which the spirals overlap each other. Continuity in the lines of the design are particularly important with this type of work, as each end has to be finished off on the back of the work to prevent it unravelling.

19

*Venor Tufting*   The *Venor Tufting* machine has very simple top threading through one set of tension plates and the needle threads from the right. The feed teeth are always in operation, the length of the feed is regulated with a knob at the front of the machine. It is designed to take candlewick yarn, heavy rug wool is a little too thick but a mixture of two-ply rug wool with other weaving yarns up to the thickness of candlewick is very satisfactory. The knee press built into the stand raises the presser foot for turning sharp corners and the large foot pedal enables a slow as well as a fast speed of 800 stitches a minute to be reached.

## Looping and cutting mechanism

The *Tufting* machine has no secondary thread and therefore no spool case. As the needle returns from its lowest point a hook is pushed between the left hand side of the needle and the loop of thread (just visible in the photograph).

The needle returns to the upper position leaving the yarn looped round the hook.
As it returns to make its second loop round the hook, the knife rises and when the needle returns to the upper position the knife cuts the first loop.

## Spool case threading and loading

The threading of spool cases is basically the same although superficially they have a different appearance. The spool must be placed the right way round in the case so that the thread cannot come out from beneath the tension spring. In order to do this the thread must be placed under the tension spring in the opposite direction from which it winds off the spool.

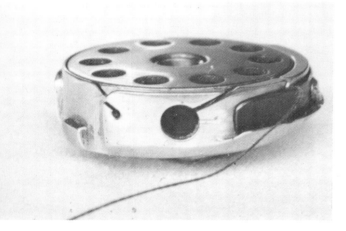

The thread comes off the spool to the right, is led through the slot and pulled back against itself under the tension spring to the left and is taken to the final outlet by being held by the left-hand thumbnail while the right hand takes it back via the right-hand slot and forwards to the exit slot.

The plan view shows the thread coming off the spool from the right and returning under the tension spring to the right, forming a loop at the first slot and making it virtually impossible to slip out from beneath the tension spring. Domestic spool cases are not as complex as the *Irish* but work on the same principle.

The view seen from the back of the *Irish* machine shows the way in which the spool case is placed into the holder. It also shows the removed presser foot bar (which was incorporated in older models) which ensures correct stitch tension. In order to release this tension when the work needs to be moved from one part of the cloth to another without cutting the top thread, the flywheel can be moved backwards and forwards by hand or the correct height for the needle must be found and held to release the thread sufficiently to draw the framed work to another position without bending or breaking the needle.

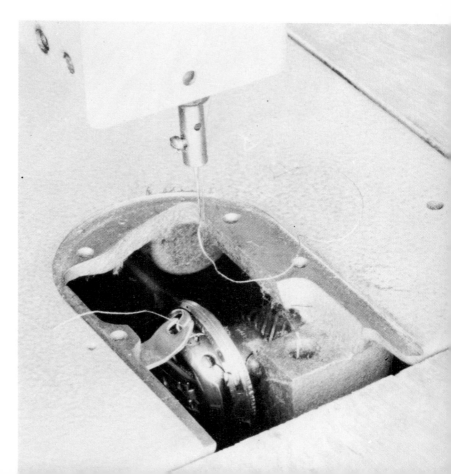

◄ The *Husqvarna* trade machine loads the spool case from the front and has a latch to prevent the spool falling out whilst being loaded.

The domestic version also loads from the front but has a spring (seen on the left of the spool case grip) which holds the spool in the same way.

The *Necchi* which loads on the left of the machine base also has a latch to facilitate loading and shows the spike at the top of the spool case which slots into the spool case holder. If the spool case is clipped firmly into this slot it prevents it from twisting round and falling out and causing trouble in the picking up of the spool thread. If the top thread does become jammed between the spool case and the holder, a latch of dark metal (seen on the right) can be released opening the ring holding the spool case in position and enabling the thread to be picked out and the spool case holder to be reassembled. This is a particularly useful aspect of the machine for beginners.

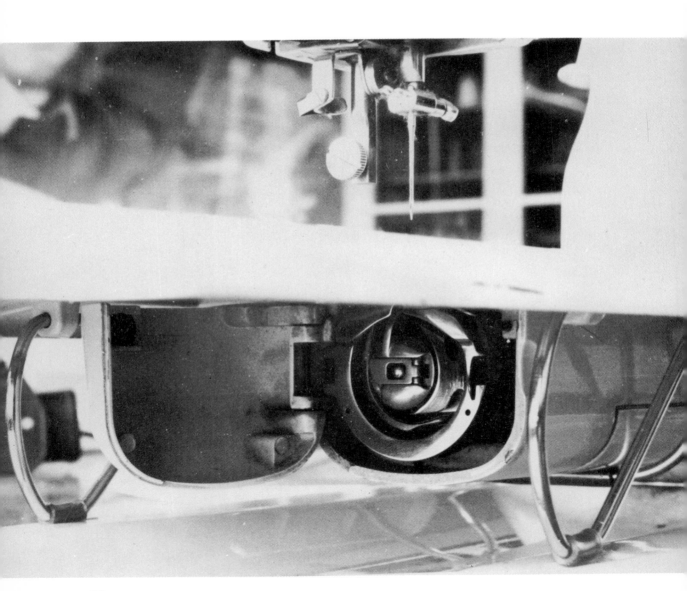

The *Bernina* has a latch for loading the machine from the front and a long spike which, when it is pushed well home, prevents the spool from dropping out. The spool case holder in this machine is particularly well constructed in that reasonable amounts of top thread finding their way into this part of the machine do not become enmeshed or cause trouble.

## Darning foot and spring attachments

All domestic machines have darning feet which can be employed without an embroidery ring when the teeth are lowered. Many of them are rather clumsy in construction making it difficult to follow the line of the needle but two types which I have found relatively successful are the ring foot on the *Bernina* and the spring employed on both the domestic and trade *Viking Husqvarna*. The previous photograph shows the position of the foot when the presser foot lever is raised.

As the needle lowers the foot rests just above the plate and remains there until the needle has moved out of the cloth when it moves up about 6 mm ($\frac{1}{4}$ in.) as can be seen most clearly in the photograph showing the lower thread brought up and twisting with the upper. This perhaps explains most clearly how the two separate threads are linked together and held when the cloth is between them.

 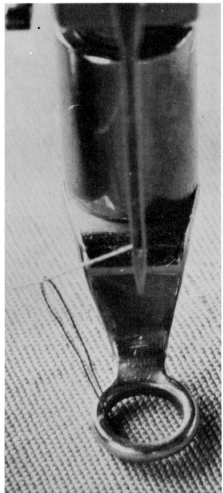

The spring used on the *Husqvarna* machines is rather easier to use as the point of the needle is still visible as it enters the cloth so that vision for free embroidery is not impeded. The spring has to be taken off to re-thread the needle which can slow things down somewhat. In both cases the top and bottom tensions have to be loosened as a certain amount of 'gathering up' can be caused by normal tensions but this is not necessary if the fabric is stretched in a frame.

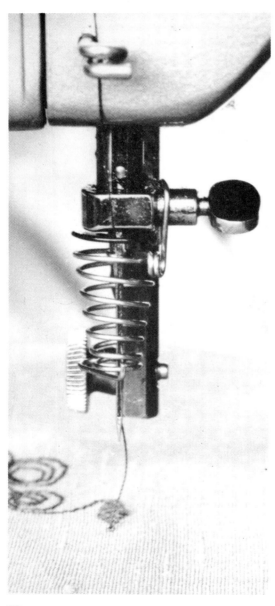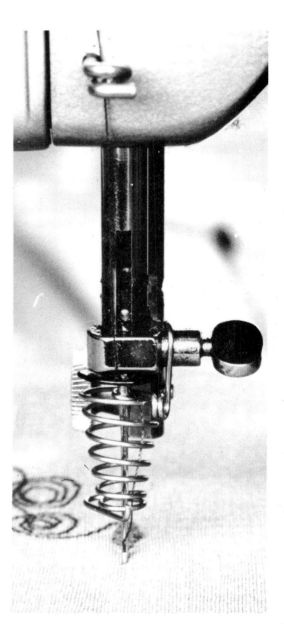

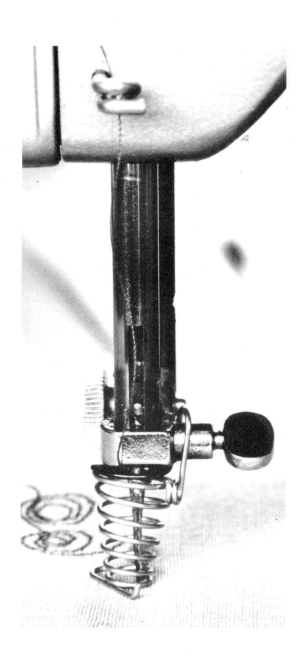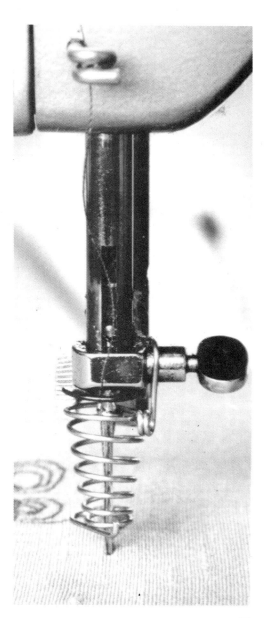

## Cover plates for special types of embroidery

The metal plates have a slot the width of the widest throw and use is made of this when an additional eyelet plate is fitted onto the domestic *Viking*. Two sizes of eyelet are possible with the two spur plates and further instructions for this appear in the next chapter. No presser foot is used as on the *Irish* machine 107W102 when Madeira embroidery is worked.

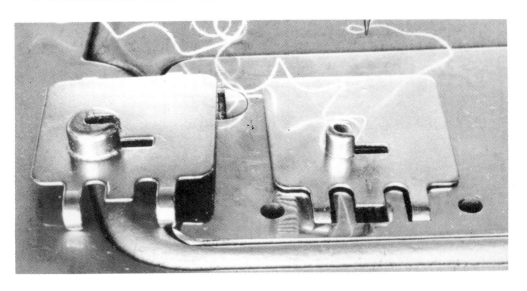

## Slow running switches

The speed at which the machine normally works is generally too fast for eyelet and parts of cut-work so that most domestic machines now have a slow as well as a high gear for working. The *Bernina* and *Necchi* both have a switch like that shown on the *Necchi* but neither produce a really slow speed. The running of the spool winding wheel against the drivewheel will slow it down a little more but this may lead to overheating the machine.

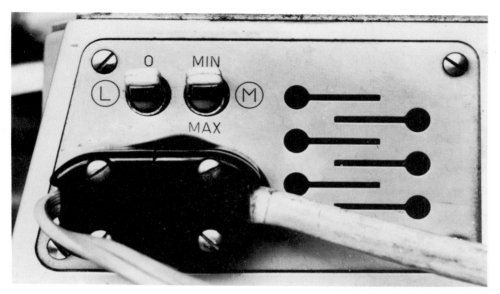

The best answer which I have found in a domestic machine is the *Viking*, where a knob is pulled onto the spool winding spindle which brings the low gear into operation. This runs the machine extremely slowly and enables the work to be turned full circle for eyelets without an unwanted build-up of stitches.

### Swing-needle levers

When buying a machine I feel the operation of the swing-needle is of paramount importance. A knee press is obviously the ideal way of operating it but if this is out of the question an easily worked hand lever is the next best thing. The width of satin stitch on most domestic machines is about 6 mm ($\frac{1}{4}$ in.), but since it is possible to encroach to obtain a greater width this need not be too big a handicap.

The narrowness of the *Necchi* lever can produce some discomfort if a great deal of shaped satin stitch is worked at one time on it. I find the round knurled knob of the *Bernina* and the large switch of the *Viking* easier to handle. The *Necchi* does, however, have two stops which can be useful in automatic pattern making allowing the lever to be moved to and fro between two pre-arranged stops without having to look at the numbers.

*Necchi*

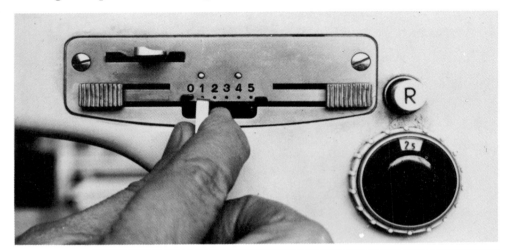

*Bernina*

## Needle position levers

All have a switch for the positioning of the needle, the *Necchi* and *Viking* have separate switches which show that shaped satin stitch, when the needle is in either of the outside positions, would have one straight edge and the other shaped. The *Bernina* had this switch conveniently placed in the centre of the swing-needle knob but it does not indicate the shape of the satin stitch. This photograph also shows the plus and minus signs used to indicate the top tension. All these machines have stitch length indicators for use with the presser foot and also reversing mechanism.

*Viking*

The *Irish* machine also have a lever mechanism at the back of the machine to govern satin stitch so that it can have one straight side and the other shaped. Since the width of satin stitch is achieved with a knee press which returns to straight stitch when the pressure is released, there is a knurled knob at the back of the machine which can be tightened on the required width of satin stitch so that lines of any width up to 13 mm ($\frac{1}{2}$ in.) can be worked.

Use of the swing needle. Rows of satin stitch encroaching in order to obtain greater width.

*Audrey Tucker*

## Presser foot bar

Most machines like the *Necchi* allow the embroidery frame to pass underneath the lowered presser foot bar when the foot has been removed. If the lever is kept lowered for machine embroidery there is no fear that the tensions will be incorrect for stitching and the same procedure for releasing the upper thread can be employed as has been suggested when working on the *Irish* machine.

## Points of difference between trade and domestic swing-needle machines

Trade machines have a higher speed of working
  a large foot pedal which makes instant control of speed possible
  a spool which holds more thread
  a greater width of satin stitch
  Trade machine needles do not have a flat edge but are completely round and are lined up with the groove at the front for threading.

## 2 Free machine embroidery on domestic machines

### Framing

Fabric (not too tight in weave) can be stretched into a 204 mm (8 in.) machine embroidery frame, which allows the whole attention to be concentrated on its movement beneath the needle. Hand embroidery frames can be used, but their greater depth makes it difficult to place beneath the needle and bar of certain machines.

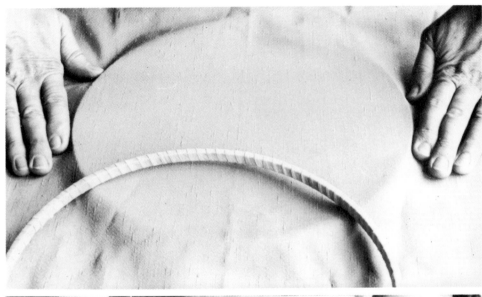

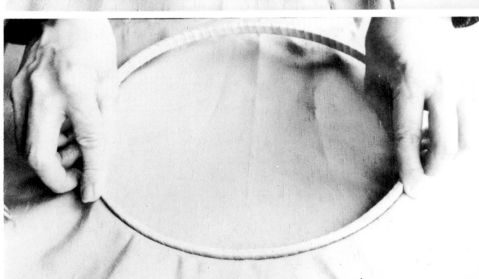

The inner ring should be bound, preferably with bandage which grips the wooden frame, to prevent the cloth from slipping. The outer ring is laid on a flat surface with the screw tight enough to allow the inner ring to fit in easily. Having tried it, remove the inner ring, place the fabric over the outer and then press the inner ring into the outer ring and towards the back of the frame.

Now press the front of the inner frame down with the heels of your hands until it is gripped by the outer.

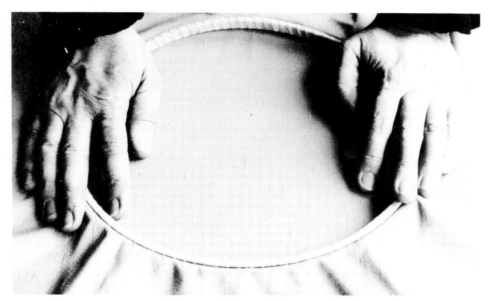

The extra slack can be tightened up by pulling the fabric over the edge of the inner frame until it is evenly stretched; that is, so that the warp and weft do not have a wriggle in them, this could cause trouble later with fine fabrics.

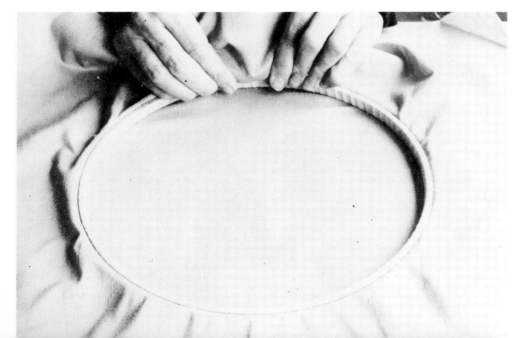

If the adjustment screw needs to be tightened it can be and the inner ring then pressed below the outer so that the fabric makes complete contact with the plate beneath the needle on the machine.

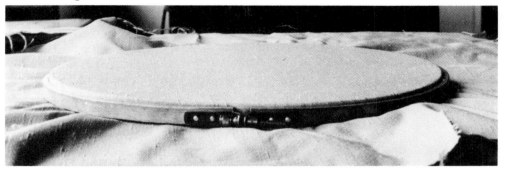

In order to keep it stretched evenly in the frame it is necessary to have fabric at least 50 mm (2 in.) larger all round than the embroidery. If the cloth is smaller than the frame, fabric of the same weight can be lapped and stitched on the right side of the work.

It is not always necessary to remove the work from the bed of the machine in order to move the frame; with practice, this can be done with the bar down, the needle either in the fabric or just above it. This prevents the finishing and starting of a great many ends of thread and is helpful in keeping a continuity in the long lines of the design.

**Varnishing muslin** is used to give body to a flimsy fabric such as chiffon and can be a substitute for a frame, keeping the fabric taught and flat with the throat plate with the aid of firm pressure by the fingers. It can also be used behind stretchy fabrics such as wool jersey to prevent them stretching too much in the frame and producing a 'cockerly' appearance to the embroidery when it is removed. It is tacked to the back of the fabric with long tacking stitches which do not interfere with the lines of the embroidery as far as possible. When the work is completed the vanishing muslin is ironed at a heat no greater than the embroidered fabric will stand, and having a low scorching point, will quickly brown and start to crumble and break up. It will disintegrate completely if the fabric is rubbed between the hands as one does to remove marks when washing. The dust can then be brushed away and the tacking lines removed.

### Threading the machine

A relaxed attitude is of great importance, so that a comfortable position, having the foot control within easy reach, should be the first consideration. When practising it is as well to use a no. 14 needle with the same or a finer thread of a different colour in the spool, so that it is easy to recognize the state of the tensions. Care must be taken that the needle is at its height when the spool is placed in the machine, so that the mechanism is in the correct position to receive it. As soon as the framed fabric is placed under the needle bar the lever should be lowered, if this has not already been done. If the lever is not lowered, the upper thread will be pulled through the fabric in loops because the tension is not engaged.

Holding the needle thread taut in the left hand, bring the drivewheel forward in an anti-clockwise direction until the needle has travelled through the fabric and returned to the top of its travel. If the needle thread is still held taut the lower thread will appear looped round the upper.

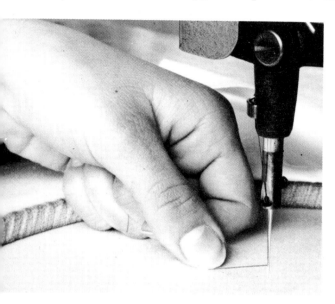
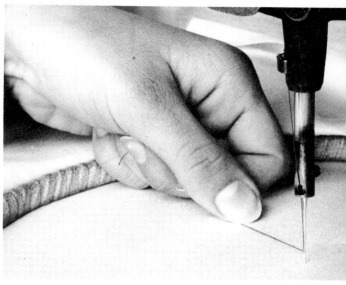
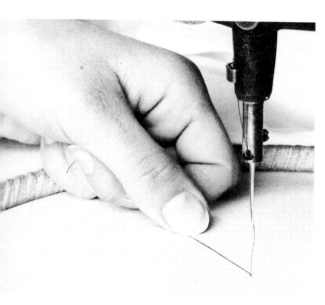
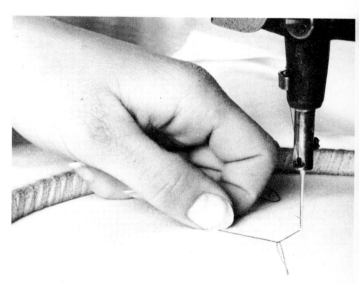

Pull the thread up onto the surface and now holding both threads in the left hand, bring the drive wheel forward again and allow the needle to enter the fabric at the same point.

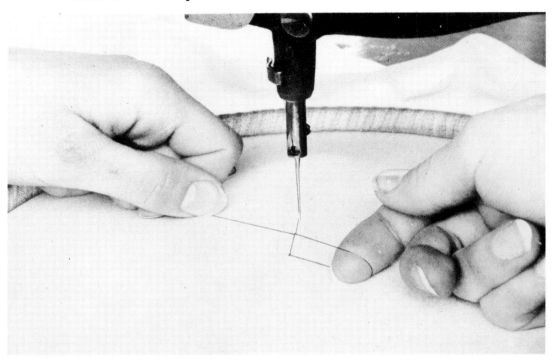

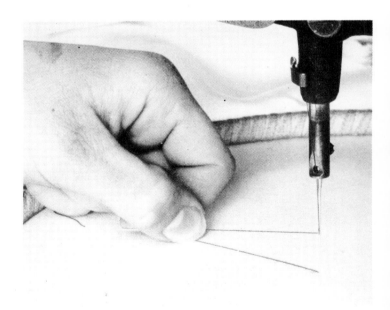

Stitch a few straight stitches before cutting the loose ends. If the lower thread is not pulled up at the first or second attempt either the fabric is not taut enough in the frame; there is a space between the fabric and the plate or the upper thread is not being held taut enough.

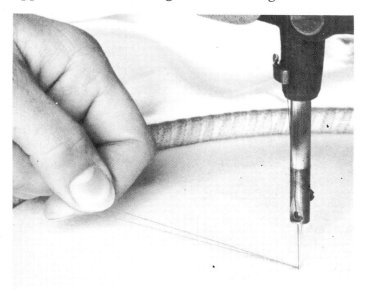

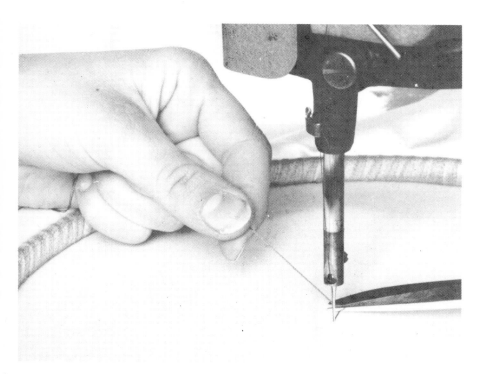

## Movement of the frame

I find that on the whole the work is best guided with the index and second fingers moving alongside the needle. The wrists should be relaxed and a certain amount of pressure should be brought to bear on the fingers so that they press firmly on the cloth.

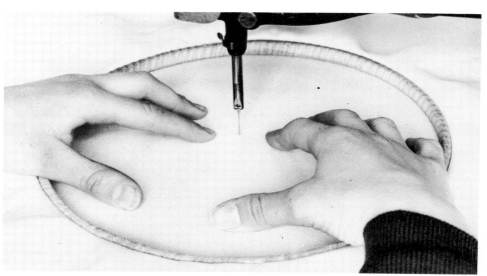

The thumbs help to guide the work whether they are on the cloth or on the edge of the frame. Where satin stitch is being worked it is best to begin and finish with a few straight stitches partly because they prevent the threads from unravelling but also because if the needle is at the top of its travel and is set to the swing position, it could come down on a finger. This is a good reason for keeping the needle bar in the centre when not expressly needed in the other two positions. It is good practice to bring the needle down near the cloth before beginning to stitch.

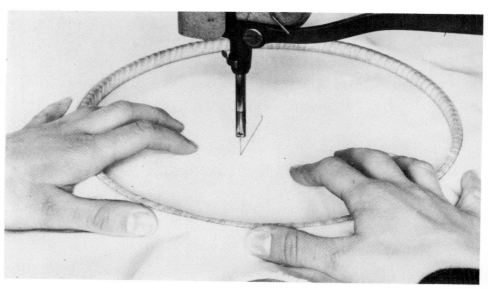

## Tensions

It will probably be necessary to alter the tensions from that for sewing to one more suitable for embroidery by loosening the top tension discs and the tension spring on the spool case. Most machines have numbered tension discs which is a great help in selecting the correct one for the thread or type of stitch. Those with signs such as the Bernina with the plus and minus need a working knowledge in positioning it.

The tension spring on the spool case is formed by a highly tempered, curved steel collar, which fits closely round the spool case and is regulated by the larger of two screws, if there are more than one, the smaller one holds it in position.

The tension can be tested by pulling the spool thread and judging the amount of tension produced by half a turn of the screw at a time. When thick threads are placed in the spool it is necessary to release the tension screw quite considerably and the danger is that this unscrews completely from the case and can be lost.

When adjusting the tension to this degree it is often best to do so over a piece of cloth so that the screw does not bounce off a hard surface and take ages to find. I have found it a good idea to keep a small supply of springs and screws for such an emergency.

### The speed of the machine

The machine should be run at a moderate, even speed; if it runs too fast, stitches will pile up on one another and the cotton will break, whilst if it runs too slowly and the frame is pulled quickly, the needle will not have time to come out of the fabric and may become bent, fraying the thread as it is drawn against the edge of the plate and eventually breaking. The frame should be moved in all directions in order to become accustomed to the unfamiliar movement and practice should be given to those movements which feel most awkward, then the uncertainty will disappear and a co-ordination between the machine and the worker will become evident. The average person feels confidence after about ten hours work, but these periods must be close together. If only two hours practice a week is achieved, progress will be slower and more difficult. The increased familiarity with the machine will soon result in a loss of nervousness for the needle and enable the fingers to move nearer it, an important step forward, since it brings a closer relation-ship with the machine, which not only works more easily but enables the embroiderer to sense more readily what the machine will do.

### Threads

Machine embroidery thread for swing-needle machines is specially made for the purpose of embroidery and so is more flexible and finer than its equivalent number in sewing cotton. It is manufactured in various thick-nesses from 100, 80 and 60 (all of which are very fine) to 50, the most usual of the finer threads to be used, and 30 which is more pliable than 50 sewing cotton but whose denier it most nearly resembles. Heavier threads can be used in the needle as long as the eye is large enough to take them, and they include sewing cotton, fine rayon and terylene. The range of threads through the spool can be thicker and besides worsted yarns, lurex plate, heavier rayon threads and hand embroidery threads can also be wound. These include coton-à-broder, star sylko (5 and 8), linen thread and up to six strands of stranded cotton. All these yarns as well as two-ply rug wool can be used on the tufting machine. The mixed threads produce an interesting texture from the variety of their length due to the varied elasticity in their make-up, mercerised cottons stretching less than silk and very much less than wool. Worsted yarns, cotton and rayon threads are all suitable for use on the *Cornelli* and *Chain-Stitch* machines and by using them in contrast to their grounds a variety of effects can be obtained, for example a worsted yarn on a rich satin or a glossy rayon on a heavy cotton.

## Needles

The sizes and types of needle vary in domestic machines although some are interchangeable. The *Singer* needle is recommended for the *Bernina* and the *Necchi* will also take a *Singer* but both it and the *Viking* machine work better with *Metwar* needles.

| NEEDLES | THREAD |
|---|---|
| | 50 sewing cotton and |
| Singer 16 | |
| Metwar 90 | 40 sewing cotton and |
| Singer 14 | silk twist |
| | |
| Singer 11 | Drima and |
| Metwar 70 | 30 machine embroidery cotton |
| | |
| Singer 9 | |
| Bernina 70 | 50 machine embroidery cotton |

Thicker threads should be wound onto the spool and the embroidery worked from the wrong side with a finer needle thread.

## Reasons for breakage of thread and lack of formation of stitch

One of the main difficulties to overcome when starting machine embroidery is the frequent breaking of the upper thread which is generally due to incorrect preparation rather than a technical fault of the machine. The following list contains reasons for this:

Failure to lower presser foot.
Incorrectly threaded machine and spool.
A blunt needle.
The machine needle too fine for the thread, which it frays.
Endeavouring to sew through too many thicknesses of heavy fabric.
The fabric set too loosely in the embroidery frame.
Allowing the machine to sew too quickly in the same place.
Moving the frame too quickly so that the thread snaps.

The following are reasons for the machine making no stitch:

The needle placed the wrong way round or set too nigh in the machine.
The needle threaded from the wrong side.

The inner ring of the embroidery frame set higher than the outer, causing a gap between the bed of the machine and the fabric so that the same piece of thread passing through the fabric several times, without being able to pick up the lower thread, eventually frays and breaks.

If none of these adjustments prevent the thread from breaking, the upper and lower parts of the machine may be 'out of time' with each other so that the spool case is not in the correct position for the thread in the needle when it is lowered to pick up that in the spool. If this is the case the needle will nearly always be found bent if not broken and the timing must be adjusted by a mechanic employed by the firm who supply the machine.

## Methods of transferring the design to fabric

### Direct tracing

Tracing the design through the cloth is the most direct method of transferring it to the fabric but can only be used for sufficiently transparent fabrics. If the design is strong enough it will be visible through a surprising number of opaque-seeming fabrics such as taffeta and lawn, especially if they contain little dye. Net or nylon need to be painted with a fine, springy sable brush using poster paint; organdie, taffeta and lawn with watercolour. A 4H pencil can sometimes be used but a fine ball point is often better since this does not mark the stitched thread like pencil and it does not stain when it is washed. A method least unlikely to mark the cloth is chalk which remains long enough on the cloth to have the main outlines stitched. It is advisable to draw only the general lines of the design as too many confuse the work and since all lines have to be covered with stitches, it will be impossible to alter the design if a further idea suggests itself. The machine will become only a means of copying onto material what has already been put down on paper, and the spontaneous quality which the machine gives will be lost. When the lines drawn onto the fabric have been worked, these will act as a guide for the embroidery which can then be worked directly with the machine, the embroiderer using the original design for reference and allowing the thread, fabric and inclination of the machine to have rather more influence on the work.

## Cut paper method

Cut paper shapes can be tacked to the fabric and machine stitched close to the cut edge, but not through the paper, which can then be removed. This means of applying the design gives simple, rather larger shapes than the cut paper and because of this direct use of the machine there is an easy transition from the original design to the embroidery. Fabric can be applied at the same time as the design is transferred to the cloth, if it is placed under the cut paper shapes before stitching. It can be cut close to the straight stitch line when the cut paper shape has been removed and the raw edge can be zigzagged.

## Pricking and pouncing

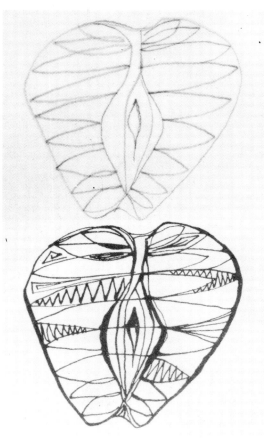

For pricking and pouncing a tracing is taken on stiff tracing paper which is pricked from the back, either by hand or slowly on the machine with a no. 9 machine needle.

This is then pinned face up on the fabric and pounce powder (resin, french chalk and/or charcoal) is pressed through the holes with the circular movement of a pad.

When the tracing is carefully removed, pounced lines on rayon can be stitched straight away as the powder does not rub off immediately.

On other fabrics the pounced lines can either be sprayed with methylated spirits and stitched to prevent them disappearing, or they can be painted with a fine brush in a tone as close to the fabric as possible in water colour or poster paint. This method allows the same tracing to be used more than once.

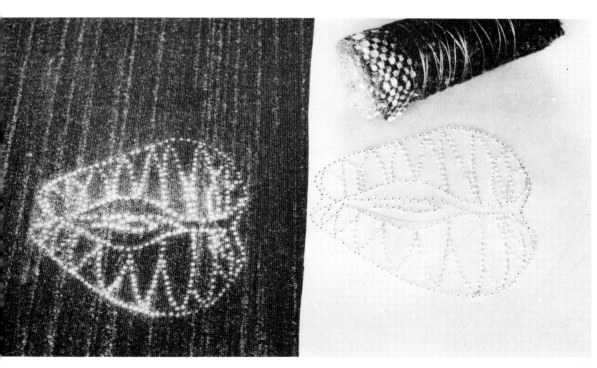

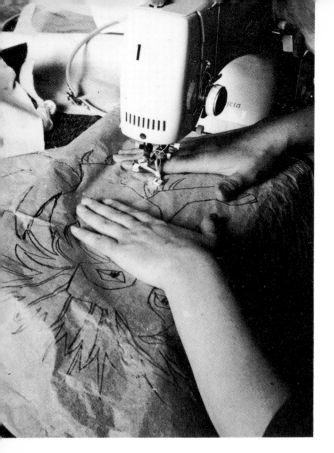

### Tissue paper tracing

A tissue paper tracing can be taken, which is tacked to the ground and the lines of the design can either be stitched to the fabric held by the darning foot attached to the machine . . .

. . . or set in a frame, and in this case the screw should be fairly tight so that when the inner ring is pressed down the fabric is taut enough to require no more pulling. This, unless done with great care, generally tears the paper. The advantage of this method is that the design can be modified by the machine as it progresses and can also be used for repetition since the original design can be used any number of times and yet remain spontaneous in execution.

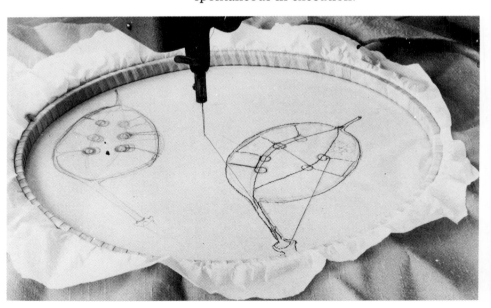

Because of the difficulty of removing paper from between two lines which are stitched close together, a simplified form of the design should be traced, and when this has been stitched, the tacking stitches can be removed and the paper torn away.

The bull was interpreted in nos 50 and 30 machine embroidery cotton on lawn. Use was made of tight top tensions and pattern suggested by the original design was used but not followed rigidly. If the design is not required to repeat, I find a direct drawing on tissue paper is best and only the main lines need be stitched. After the tissue is torn away one cannot be influenced by the drawing and the transition to the embroidery is more direct.

## Direct working

This method of working directly from the design or object onto the fabric with the machine, enables an interpretation of the idea to be made rather than a copy and is productive of a spontaneous approach. It also enables different interpretations to be tried and it is often in this searching for form that character and life are revealed. It is also a sure way of searching out poor design material.

# 3  Designing with the machine

When designing machine embroidery the characteristics of the machine must be taken into consideration as they form an integral part of the work. In the first place it must be remembered that it is the needle which is static and the fabric which moves. There is a tendency, since the machine gives a line, to consider it another form of drawing instrument, like the pen or pencil, but if it is only used for this purpose it will have disappointing results. As the primary production of the machine is texture, this can be exploited to the full by the use of tensions and threads. Unlike the pencil, which when it has completed a line can be removed from the paper to make another, the free thread cannot move easily about the fabric, and in releasing it the rhythm of working is lost. This would suggest that the greater the continuity in the lines of the design the better.

## Automatic stitching

A great deal can be done in a decorative way with the automatic setting of the machine by the use of automatic stitch patterns which are explained in the manual of each machine, but a variety of line and texture is possible without this. The straight stitched line can be given a different appearance either in the variety of its length or in the type of thread used.

In the case of soft floss wound on to the spool and held tightly by the upper thread, a cable stitch is achieved.

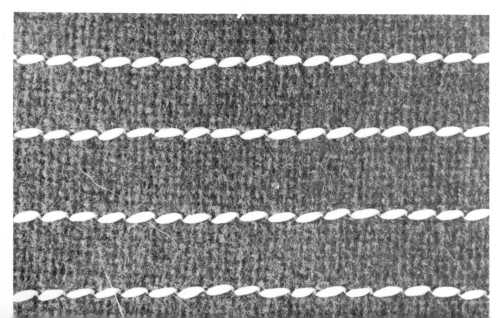

A further difference is produced by an alteration in the tension of the upper thread, so that initially a curved stitch is formed in being pulled by the lower thread through the fabric but as the upper tension increases the thread sits on the surface of the cloth in a straight line.

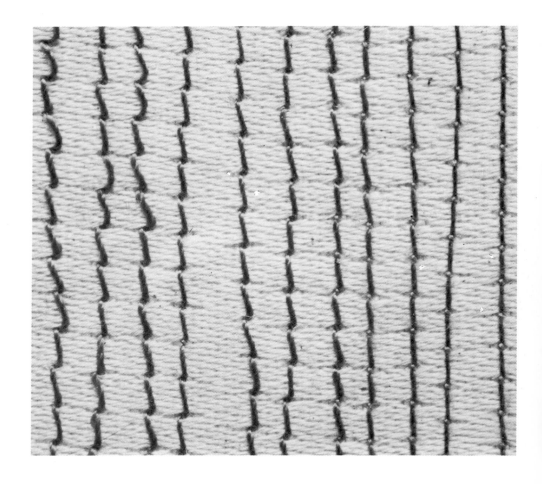

Unequal tensions and length of zigzag also produce a varied appearance to the stitch and further differences can be achieved by the use of the same, slightly different and tonally opposed threads of the same or differing denier.

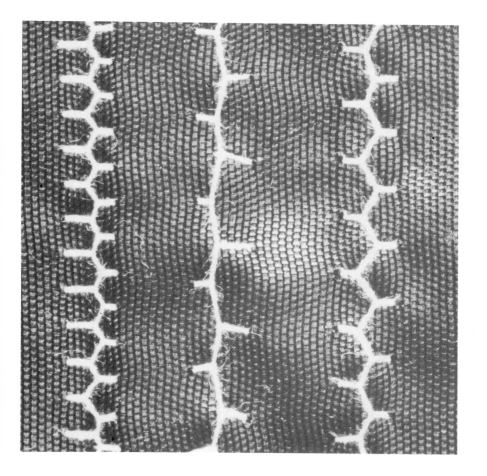

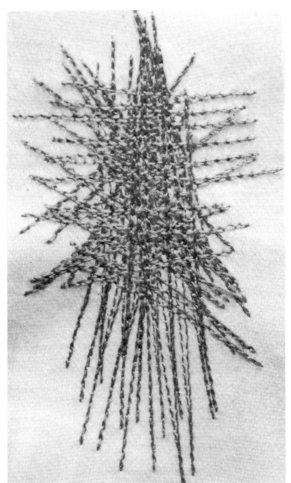

Areas of texture can be achieved by cross-hatched straight stitch lines either by working lines in rows, turning at the end of each to remain parallel or by using the reverse gear to go backwards and forwards. In this case the tensions must be reduced to prevent puckering.

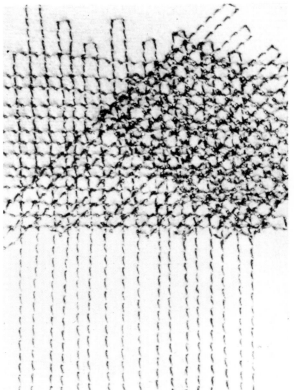

Cross-hatching worked in zigzag gives rather different texture, almost obscuring the cloth in certain areas if it is worked diagonally as well as horizontally and vertically.

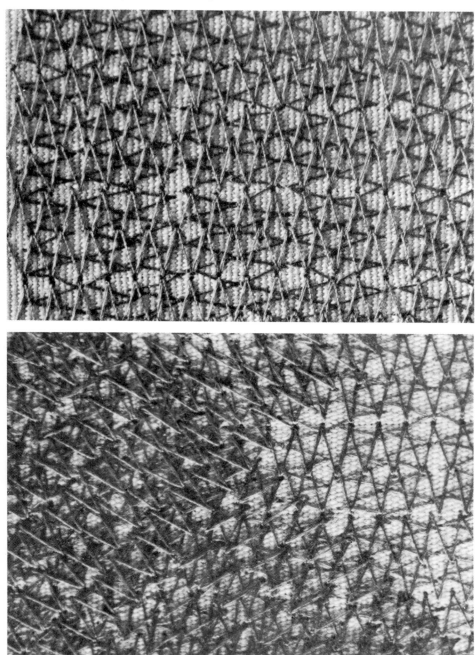

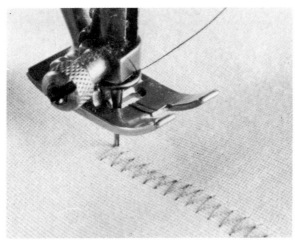

It should be possible for the second row of stitching to form diamonds with the first, the needle going into the hole made by the previous stitch, if however the line wanders even fractionally away from the previous row the zigzag will become slightly staggered as can be seen in the first two lines of stitching. If this irregularity is not desirable, a transparent presser foot can be used.

▲

At the end of the first zigzag row the needle has to be on that side of the presser foot nearest the part to be stitched so that when the foot is lifted and the work turned 180 degrees with the needle still in the cloth it will stitch over the correct area. If at the end of the second turn this is not done you will find yourself zigzagging over the first row of stitching.

▼

When all the rows in the first layer of stitching have been done the needle remains on the 'outside' edge of the work so that when it is turned 90 degrees it is in the correct position to stitch over the previous rows at right angles.

The same process is followed until the whole of the area is filled. The unevenness of 'cover' may also be due to the ribbed nature of the cloth and if a greater accuracy is demanded a smoother cloth might help. A regular 'star' pattern can be produced and may be useful at times, but its very regularity can produce an unbalanced element in freer work.

Further rows can be worked diagonally as in cross-hatching, in fact the build-up of rows of zigzagging is limited only by the demands of the design and the number of thicknesses of thread through which the needle will go without fraying the needle thread. By using the reverse and forward movement of the machine zigzag areas of texture can be worked in lines and cross-hatching.

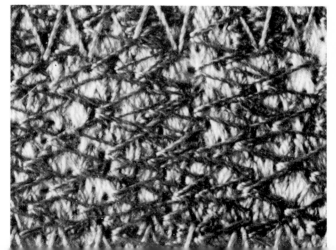

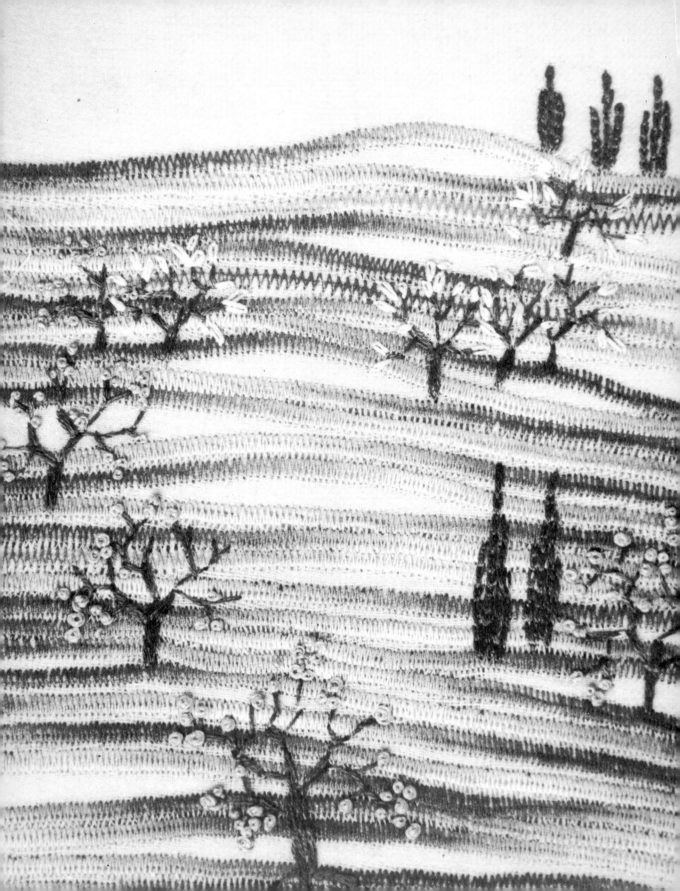

◄ The background of this panel has been achieved by using the presser foot. Lines of zigzag of equal width have been worked in a very free flowing manner, some encroaching upon each other to produce a more solid texture, others allowing lines of the ground to remain visible. A slight variety in the length of stitch has been used, in some cases nearly close enough to produce satin stitch and holes and some lines of open work have been retained in the soft rather loosely woven cloth by the tightness of the tension.

*Goldsmiths'   Anne Vaughan*

## Twin needle

The twin needle has been used to produce lines of tucking on nuns veiling by increasing the lower tension. Some tucks have been stitched next to one another, others leaving a channel of fabric.

*Goldsmiths'   Anne Vaughan*

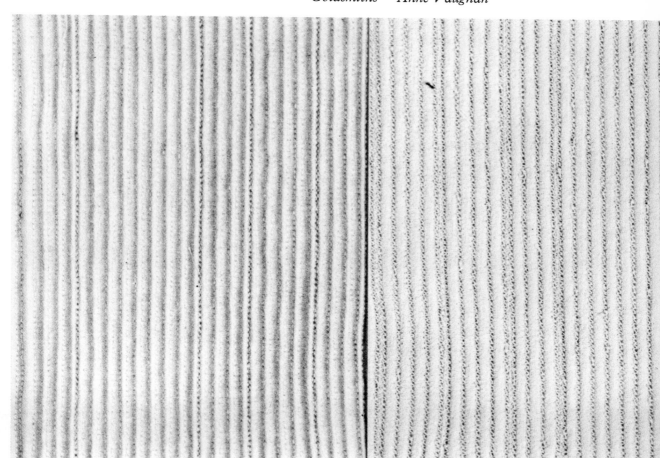

Two different coloured threads have been used here in the twin needle, emphasizing the raised quality which the tight lower tension gives. Thick cords have been sewn down with an open zigzag so that it does not obscure the nature of the yarn and thick spool threads have been corded.

*Judy Barry*

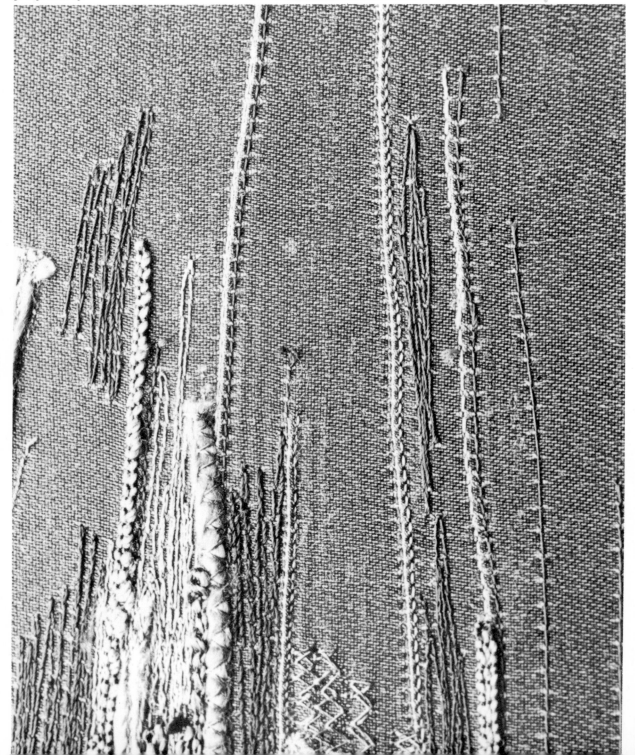

## Tufting

Tufting is worked from the back leaving a stitched line whilst the tufted loop is cut by the machine as it works. A variety of wool and linen or cotton threads gives tufts of different lengths since the wools with their elastic quality stretch on the hook more than the cottons and when cut are shorter in length.

The tacking foot on the *Bernina* also provides tufting using fine cotton threads which have been used here. Mossing on the *Cornelli* has been used to give another texture and the principle of the twin-needle has been used for the padding of two parallel stitched lines for Italian quilting.

*Manchester    Helen Lord*

## Quilting

Both Italian and English quilting can be worked with the foot. In English quilting the pressure on the presser foot bar will have to be released to accommodate the padding and to make it easier to turn curves smoothly. The use of the foot is an asset in Italian quilting in order to maintain parallel lines. This is best backed with an open muslin so that the padding thread can be introduced easily.

Parallel padded lines have been used on the panel and have been worked by the English rather than the Italian principle.

*Julie Graham Rogers*

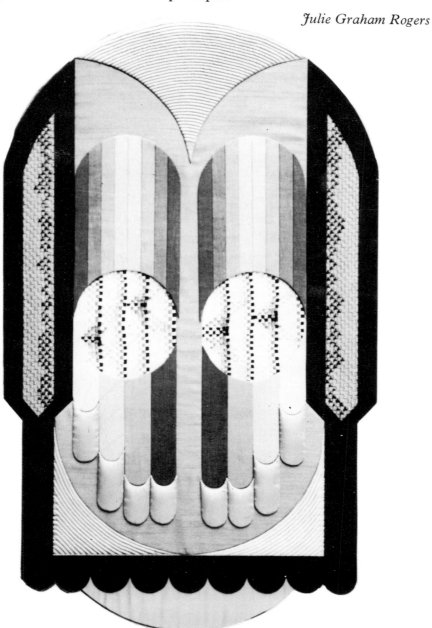

69

## Free machine embroidery

This is the term usually applied to machine embroidery worked without the feed teeth moving the work. This is lowered and the work moved by hand either with the hands alone pressing the fabric down firmly onto the throat plate or with the aid of a darning foot or a frame to keep the fabric taut. This enables curves to be made more easily than is possible with the normal presser foot and increases the flexibility of the line.

### Suggestions for beginners

I would recommend the use of a round frame to begin with since this not only keeps the fabric taut but gives one something firm to hold on to. A stout needle no. 14 with no. 30 machine embroidery thread should prevent the needle from breaking (unless very roughly used) or the thread from breaking if all the precautions mentioned in the previous chapter have been taken. A fine cotton fabric can be used to work on as long as the weave is not so fine that the needle sticks in it as it is drawn in and out. The tensions should be equal to start with and it will probably be found necessary to relax these after the machine has been set for sewing with the presser foot.

To begin with small curves and spirals can be worked so that the frame is being moved in all possible directions. When this can be done without jerking, the size of these curves can be varied to encourage greater dexterity in the manipulation of the frame. In your state of tension (which most beginners have) try not to press too hard on the power foot, this will make it appear that the machine is running away with you. It is not, of course, possible for it to do so as the feed-teeth are not engaged, but if the fabric is moved slowly to 'compensate', the build-up of thread in one spot will lead to the needle thread breaking. This is one of the main frustrations for beginners and can be avoided to some extent if you are able to relax and allow the machine to work at a moderate speed. It is a good idea to have a different coloured spool and needle thread and it is sometimes a help if the spool thread is finer. In allowing spirals to overlap, variations in texture will be made, large patterns will give a light texture merging into the ground, whilst small, overlaid spirals will form a dense area with a matt appearance.

Both overlapping and open spirals have been worked in a short stitch so that a great many stitches have been used to form each spiral in order to obtain the maximum curve. In this case the machine was working at a moderate to fast speed and the work was moved slowly.

At the opposite end of the scale the machine worked slowly and the frame ▶ was moved quickly to produce this pattern. Care has to be taken that in moving the frame quickly the needle is not bent but it is possible to build up a particular rhythm which prevents this. The angular quality so different from the smooth curves of the previous pattern produces quite a different texture.

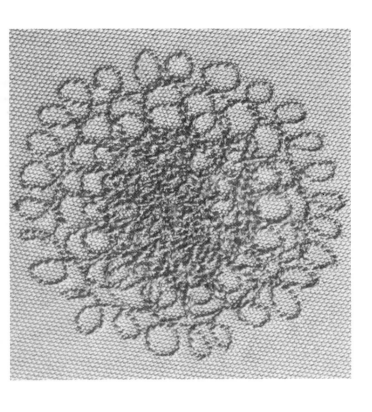

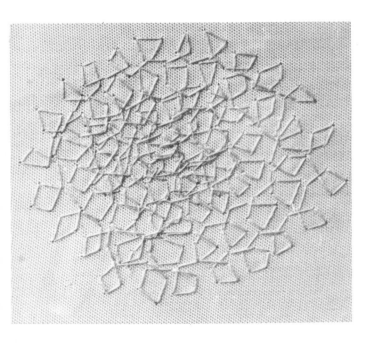

## Tensions

*Whipping*   By tightening the upper tension it is possible to bring the lower one up just sufficient to whip it. The upper one becomes a crisp line lying on the surface of the cloth whilst the lower, if different in tone can alter its tonal appearance by the length of the stitch employed. In this case a long stitch hardly alters the appearance of the top thread when it occasionally couches it but covers it completely when the stitch is shortened to allow a build-up of lower over upper thread.

In order to allow more lower thread to come through, the tension spring on the spool case can be released and in pulling the fabric quickly round in spirals the upper thread is tightened even more, pulling the lower through. No. 30 machine embroidery thread has been used in both spool and needle giving a heavier appearance than a finer spool thread would.

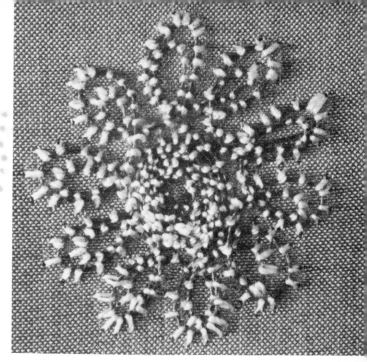

As the spiral extends in size this brings up the lower thread in longer loops without altering the spool tension.

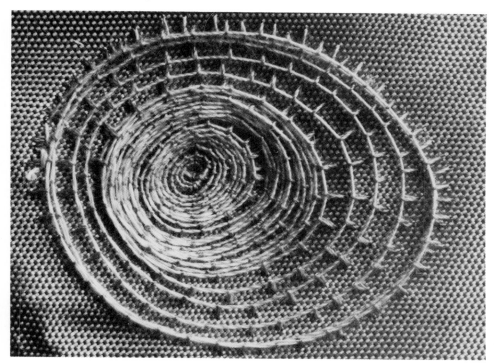

If the lower tension is relaxed very considerably and the upper tightened sufficiently for it not to bend the needle or break the thread a very three dimensional spiral can be achieved with the inner rows supporting and lifting the threads of the outer.

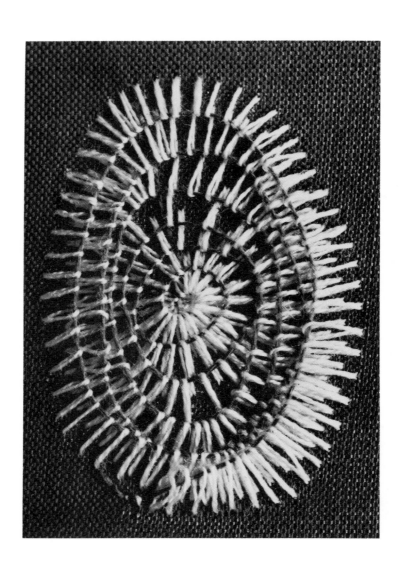

Here large loops and very tight spirals cover the ground for the foliage of a panel.

*Judy Barry*

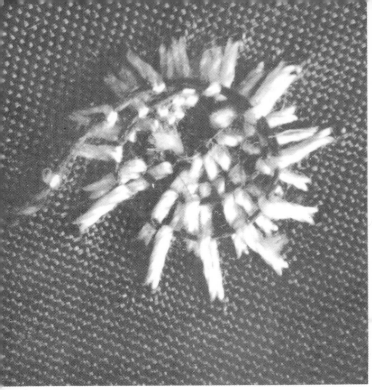

Small raised spots can also be built up if the lower thread is loose enough.

'Ends' and finishing off can be a considerable ▶ problem so that the use of this method as a continuous line to give a textured ground helps to overcome this. There is a difference in appearance in the use of no. 30 and no. 50 machine embroidery cotton, the 30 tending towards slightly larger spirals and being rather richer in weight, the 50 giving a more lacy appearance.

If these are to remain separate from each other the upper thread at the end of each spiral needs to be finished when all the spirals have been worked. The thread can be snipped close to the point at which it enters the centre of a fresh spiral and threaded through to the back of the work with a hand needle.

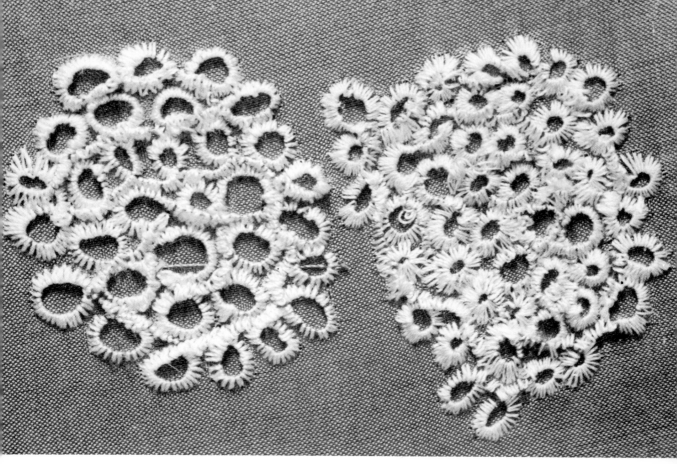

A further difference can be achieved by the use of a dark instead of a light thread.

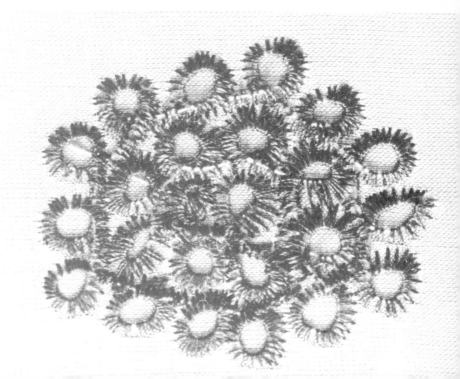

More formal continuous borders also lend themselves to this method, producing a rich effect quickly. The original line of stitching can be seen from the holes in the cloth but the line of which we are most strongly aware is the taut upper thread making a continuous loop on the surface.

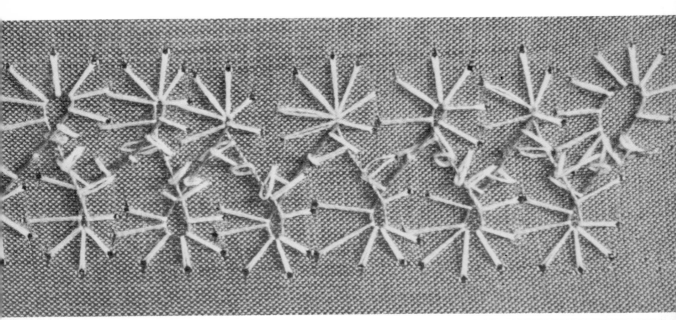

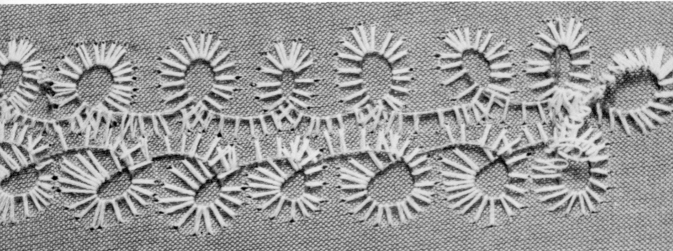

The more spikey border is produced by moving the fabric more quickly, but with this speed, control of shape and tensions is less reliable. With practice this could be overcome. The spool tension has been tightened and a 30 machine embroidery cotton used in the spool, it is obviously happier with the curve than the spike but here again greater understanding of the abilities of the machine and its tensions will improve performance.

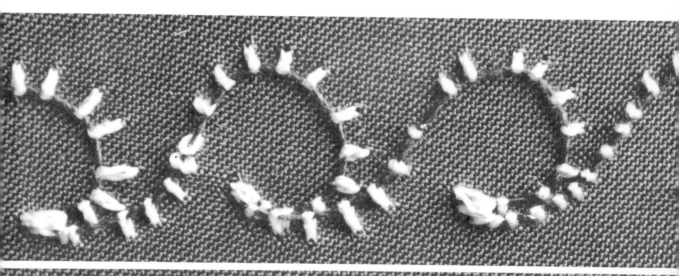

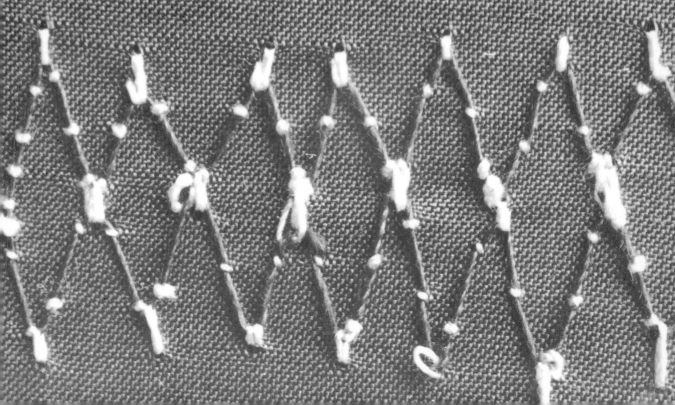

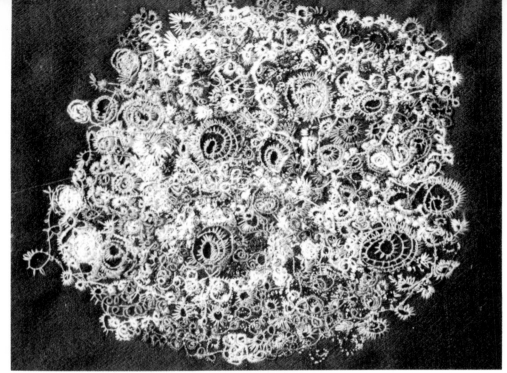

*Goldsmiths'   Judith Standeven*

The richness of a ground can be increased by the use of different tones and colours. It is also interesting to note the very different appearance of these two whipped areas, the loose lacy appearance of one against a dark ground and the more 'pebbly' treatment of the other with a less tight top tension and without such a strong tonal contrast on its light ground.

*Goldsmiths'   Judith Standeven*

A very definite contrast in spool and top thread has been used here with a tight top tension. The continuous spirals almost completely cover the muslin ground which has become distorted into raised mounds by the tightness of the tension like the split stitch cheeks of *Opus Anglicanum* figures. Some of these have been padded from the back to retain their raised form.

*Judy Barry*

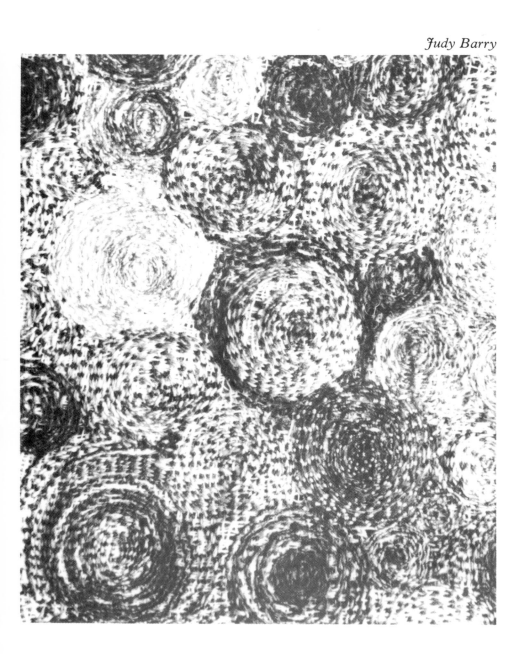

## Shadow work

With a tight lower and a loose upper tension the looped threads can be seen through transparent fabric. A spiral technique seems necessary in order to pull the loose thread taut so that enough of it can be seen and where colour is used the muteing of it by the muslin or organdie will increase the accent made by the stitching round the edge of the spiral. There is no reason why this should not be worked from the back if a tight upper tension is preferred for working.

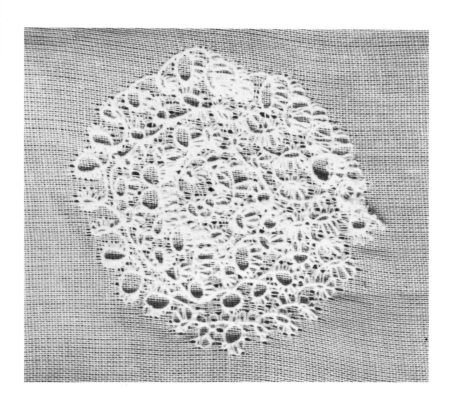

*Drawn fabric*

With a tight upper and lower tension and using a wide needle throw, it is possible to pull the loosely woven threads of linen scrim or hessian together so that open channels and holes are formed in its ground. No threads have been cut but have been gathered together within the stitching. Some of the horizontal background threads have been whipped, others have been left to form a lacy texture.

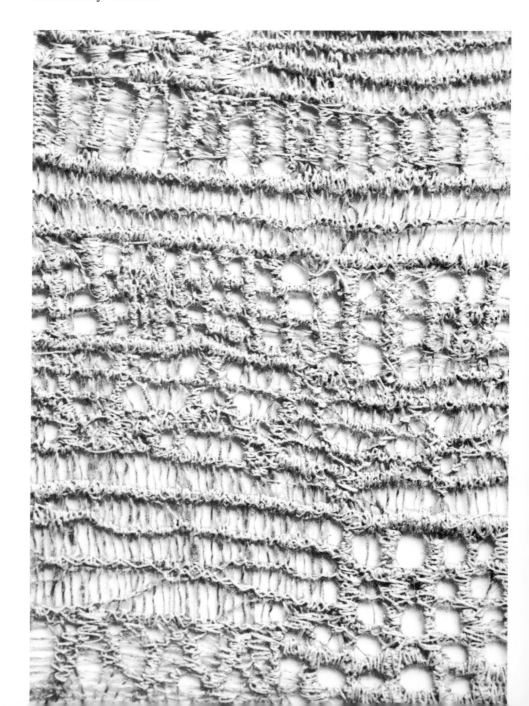

## Gathering

A form of quilting without a backing fabric has been produced by tight tension on soft felt without the use of the frame to keep the fabric taut. This has been encouraged to gather until a relief surface has been achieved.

*First Year Dip AD Manchester*

## Cable stitching

Thick threads which will not go through the needle are placed in the spool, the tension spring being relaxed considerably. It is worked from the back either in a frame or tacked to vanishing muslin. The lower thread must be brought to the surface and to do this it is best to use a heavy machine sewing cotton in the needle, which is stout enough to make a large enough hole; nos. 14 or 16 would probably be best. If the lower tension is loose enough to be pulled through the cloth by the strong upper cotton and the yarn is soft in character, the 'beading' effect of cable stitch will be produced. A more rigid effect will be produced if a firm yarn such as linen is placed in the spool and a fairly tight tension used on the spool so that the upper thread is dragged through, couching the spool thread which rests on the 'right side' of the cloth.

The machine should run at a moderate speed whilst the fabric is moved quickly and firmly if a taut couched line is required.

This has been done here with a variety of threads. Different spool tensions have also been used for the floss threads and in some cases the work has been moved slowly so that the spool thread has looped.

*Judy Barry*

86

In this one not only has a loose lower tension been used but a great deal of over stitching has been employed.

*Goldsmiths'   Judith Standeven*

## Cording and couching

Both trade and domestic machines have cording attachments. These allow the swing-needle to zigzag over an auxiliary thread held in position over the throat plate. Domestic machines employ a foot which may also necessitate the use of the feed-dog but the *Irish* machine allows the work to be held in a frame.

The *Cornelli* employs a foot. Here both straight and looped yarns have been corded.

*Judy Barry*

If the corded and auxiliary yarns to be stitched down are held by hand or tacked down in some manner without the aid of a cording foot or corder, I have distinguished them by the hand embroidery term *couching*. If the 'threads' are thick and soft enough they can be straight stitched, particularly if they are too wide for the throw of a domestic machine.

The *Necchi* darning foot was used in the embroidery of the lion, the cords being placed on last.

*Hull    June de Vries*

Auxiliary threads can also be held down in a decorative way with line stitching as can be seen in this example of whipping over lines of soft wool.

*Gay Swift*

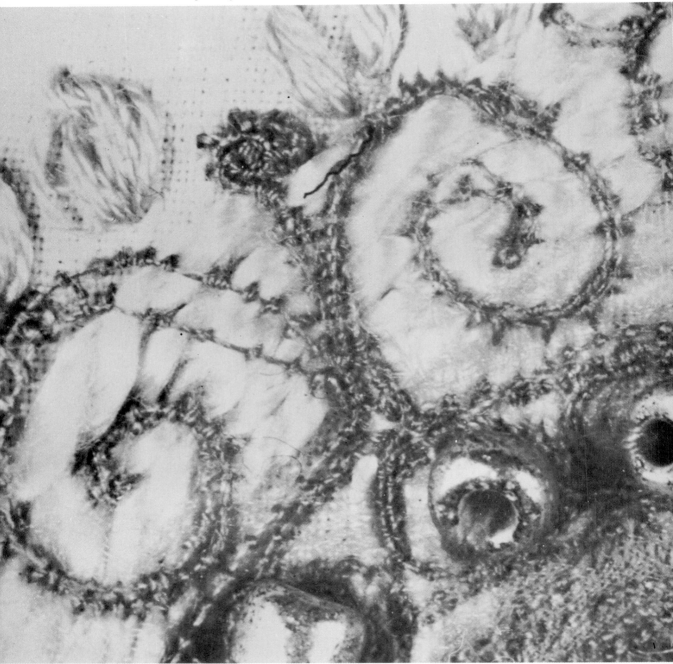

The couched threads themselves can be partially untwisted and stitched down with straight and zigzag so that the couching thread is partly masked by the couched thread.

*Judy Barry*

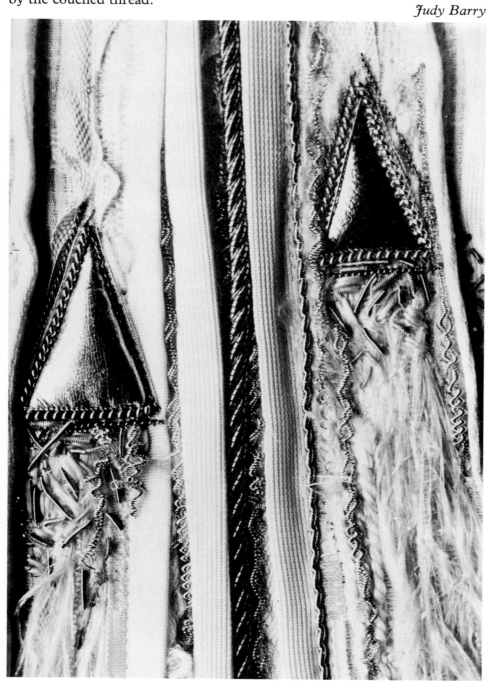

The couching thread itself if worked in satin stitch can entirely cover the padding thread so that it is raised considerably from the ground. Here the effect of the padded satin has been increased by the use of glossy and matt threads as well as being used in conjunction with gold cords, pearl-purl and kid. If the needle throw is sufficiently wide, rope can be used for padding as it does not squash flat when stitched, but the upper tension will have to be relaxed quite considerably in order that the lower tension is not brought up and a smooth satin finish is produced. The upper tension is generally better slightly loose for all couching unless the lower thread is brought up deliberately to give an edge to the couched thread. If the full width of the couched thread is to be held by the zigzag, the throw can be a little wider than the thread which can also be twisted as it is stitched down to prevent it being flattened.

*Judy Barry*

*Perspex* or *Plexiglass* rods have been held in place with net and veiling placed over them and then stitched on either side to keep them in place.

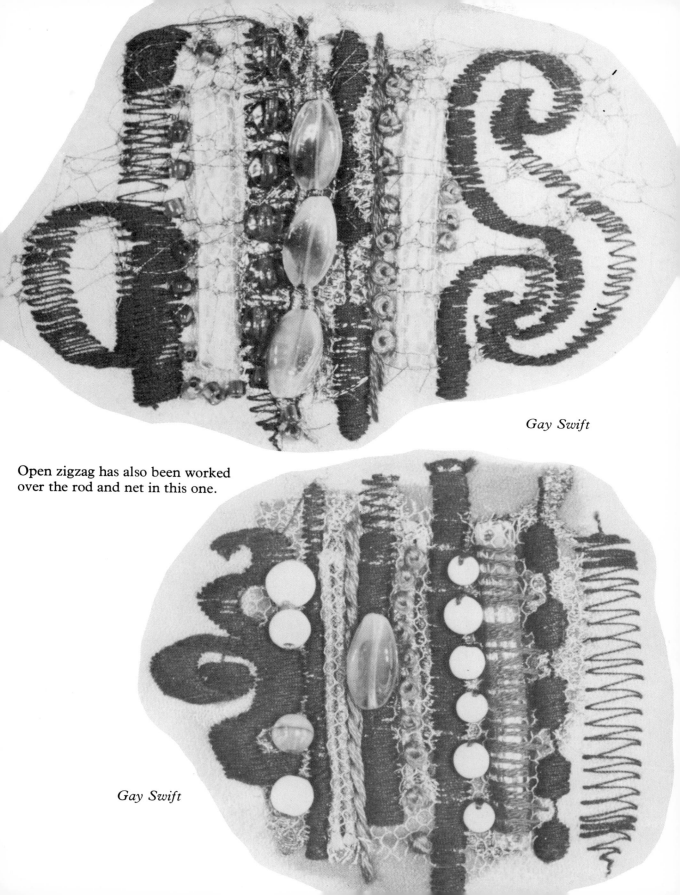

*Gay Swift*

Open zigzag has also been worked
over the rod and net in this one.

*Gay Swift*

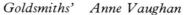

Satin stitch

The appearance of this varies according to the length of the stitch, that is whether the stitches are allowed to pile up against one another in satin stitch or the fabric is moved quickly in relation to the speed of the machine, producing an open zigzag.

In this sample a constant width of satin stitch has been worked horizontally and vertically with the same thread which produces a dramatic tonal change. The felt has been moved backwards and forwards as well as sideways without turning except 90 degrees for the over stitching.

*Goldsmiths'    Anne Vaughan*

In this a variety of widths of satin stitch have been used and the ground has been covered by encroaching satin stitch as well as rows worked next to one another. The introduction of a lurex spool thread adds another quality to the texture.

*Goldsmiths'    Anne Vaughan*

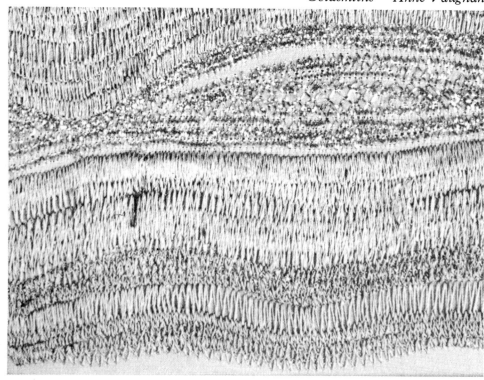

This method of encroaching can be used on domestic machines where the greatest satin stitch width is narrower than trade machines. This can either be worked in a succession of encroaching lines or in rows next to one another with a joining row worked on top.

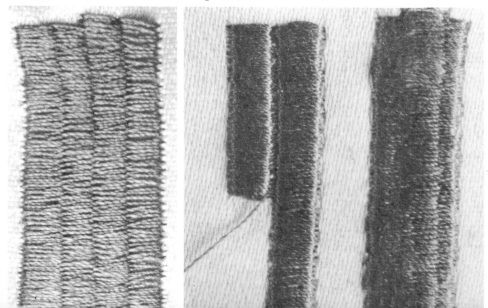

Satin stitch can be worked diagonally to produce a spikey effect not unlike stem stitch, or over and over itself to produce raised satin stitch spots. Here they have been stitched at a variety of angles to produce the greatest tonal effect from the same thread. The 'beaded' effect has been heightened in certain places with straight stitch round the outside of the satin, this also rounds off square blocks if the satin stitch spot is not shaped.

PLATE I    Detail from a door curtain worked on dark grey flannel. Hessians, silks and gold tissue have been applied and the forms further decorated on the Irish machine with line and satin stitch    *Gillian Dick, Hull*

*Judy Barry*        *Judy Barry*

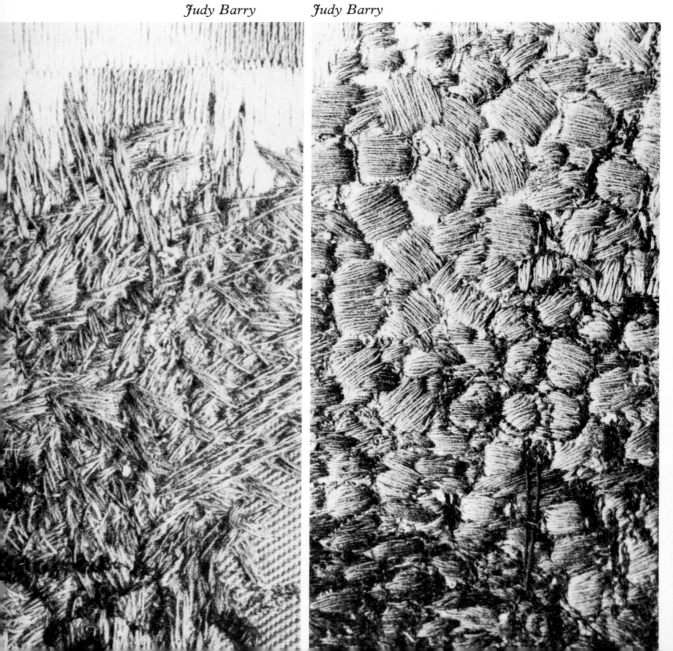

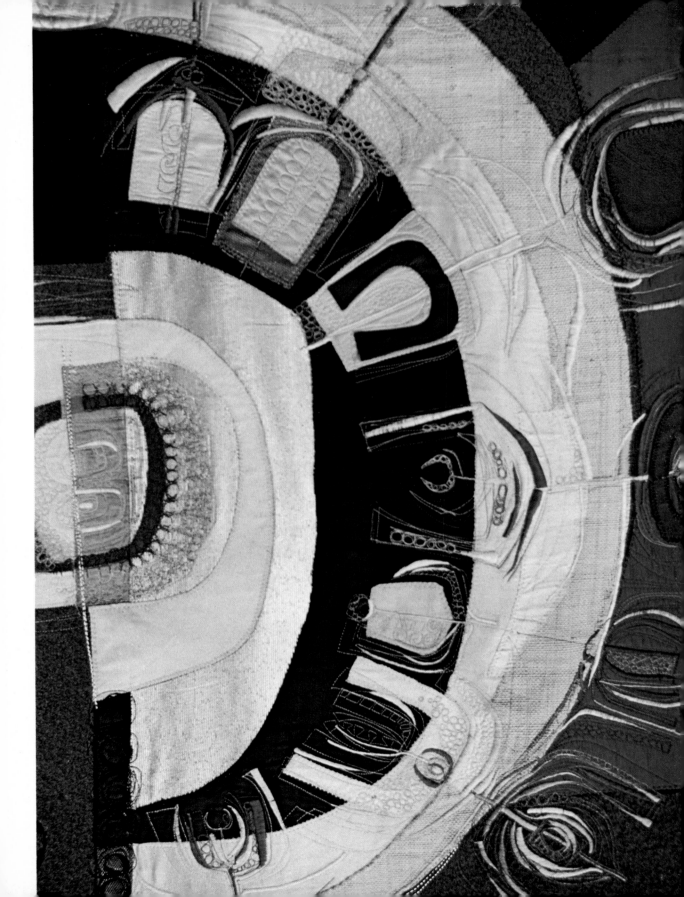

Shaped satin stitch spots have been worked over a bar of satin stitch to produce a further three dimensional quality. Worked on a trade machine with a knee press this is fairly simple but some practice will be necessary with the hand lever on a domestic machine in order to produce sensitively shaped satin stitch.

*Gay Swift*

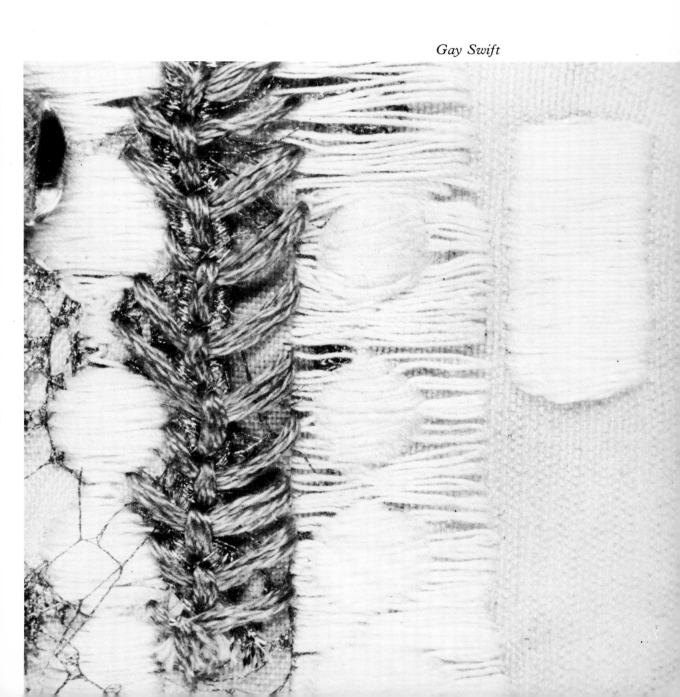

Here some satin stitch blocks have been cut with the unpicker to produce a tufted velvet texture, very rich against the smooth satin stitch.

*Manchester    Helen Lord*

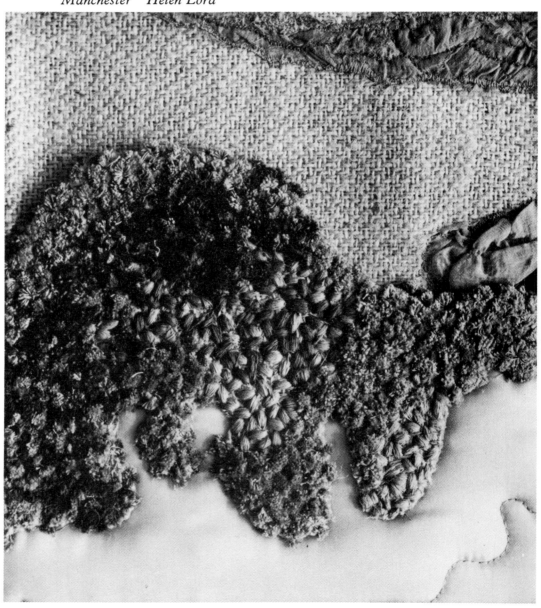

Longer tufting has been achieved with the *Bernina* tacking foot. Its tactile quality has been increased by its placing near the smooth encroaching satin. The rough satin stitch has been achieved by bringing up the lower thread and mossing has been used to give a looped instead of a cut tuft.

*Manchester    Helen Lord*

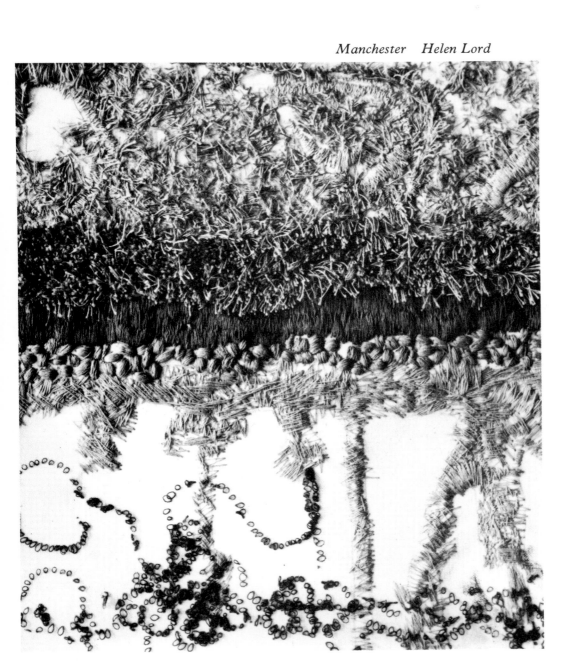

Heavier threads can be used on the tufting machine and here mercerized and matt cottons have been used.

*Manchester   Julie Graham Rogers*

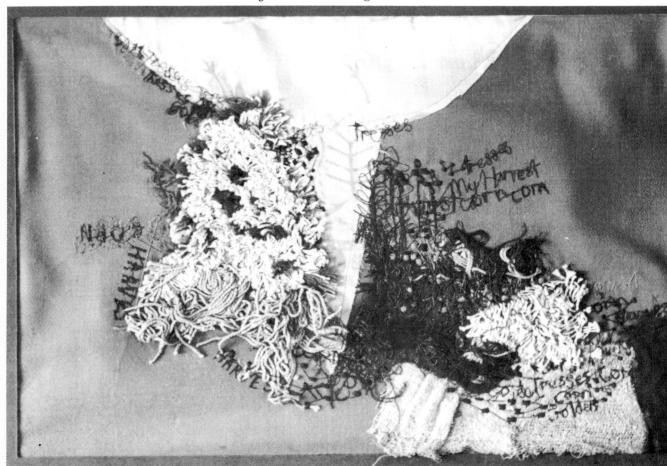

Chain stitch

The *Cornelli* is rather more limited than the *Irish* machine since it relies on the production of lines for its effect, the appearance of the line can however be altered, dependent upon the type of thread used and the length of stitch. It can be used to produce bold line or texture of linked chain or detached loops. Continuous line is an advantage in the design since all ends must be finished off on the wrong side to prevent unravelling. A change in the direction in which the chain stitch lies produces a syntillation from glossy threads as well as metal ones.

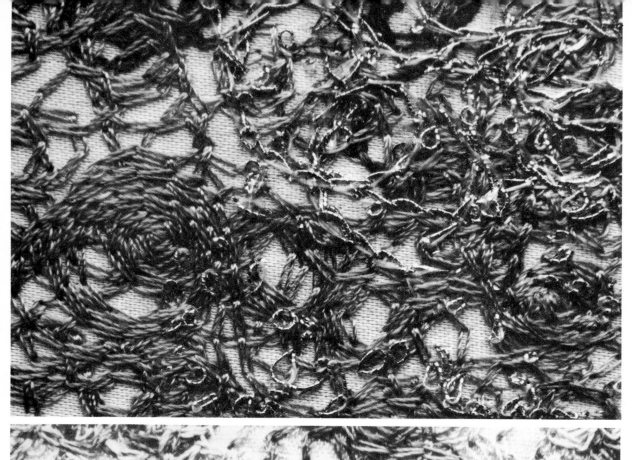

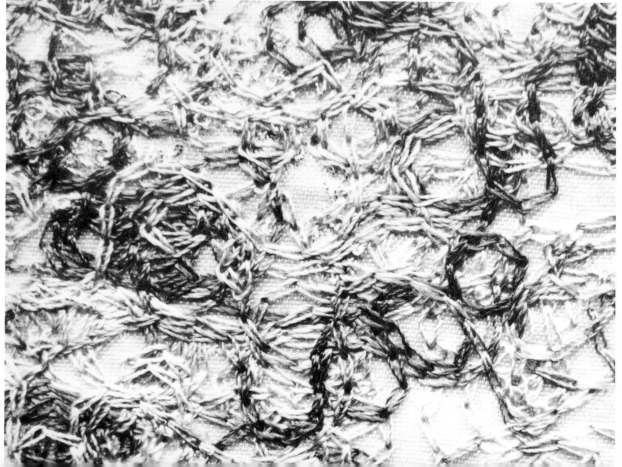

The production of moss stitch as a looped texture is possible on the domestic machine if a very loose lower thread whips the upper which can then be withdrawn leaving the loops on the surface. It is as well to work on a fairly closely woven fabric which will grip the loops and prevent them slipping out. *Stayflex* could be ironed to the back of the work when it is finished if necessary to prevent this.

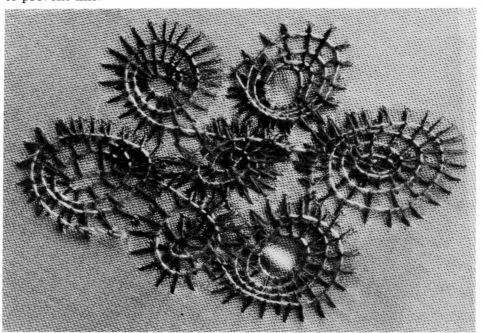

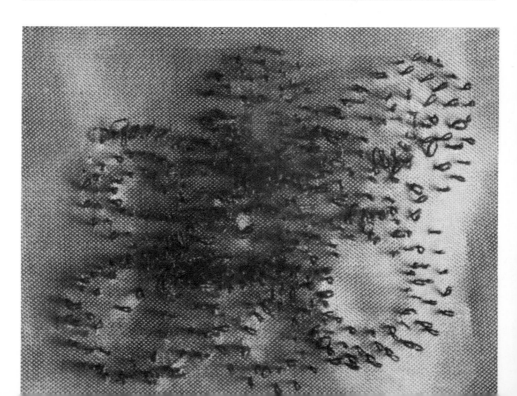

## Cut-work

The series of stages in cut-work have been shown here worked on organdie stretched firmly in a frame with no. 50 machine embroidery cotton and a fine needle.

Three rows of stitching are worked first.

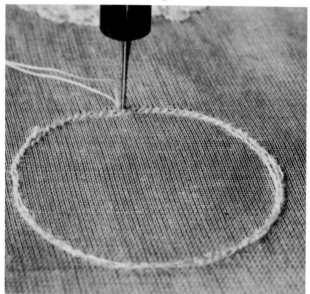

A fourth line is then stitched round to the right-hand quarter . . .

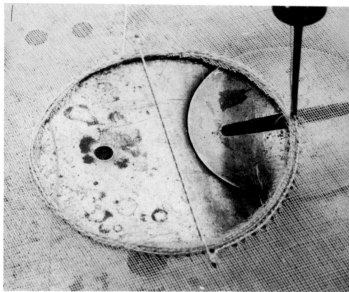

The fabric inside cut away, and then with the needle at the far side, the fabric is pushed away bringing the needle and thread to the near side whilst driving the motor at a moderate to fast speed. The faster the speed of the motor the more tightly twisted the two threads will be.

when the fabric is turned and two or three stitches are worked to prevent the first rows of stitching pulling away from the main fabric when the next bar is worked. This cuts the first one in half . . .

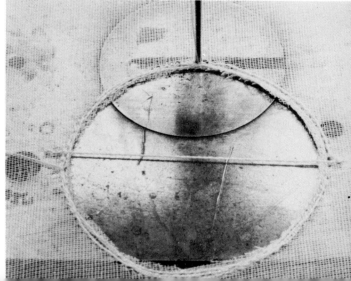

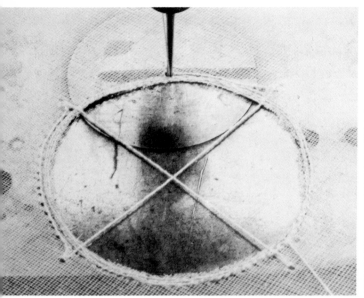

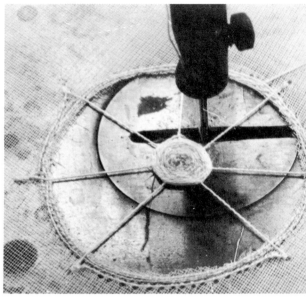

. . . and continues to the nearside making a stitch into the fabric and then round the outside for an eighth. This bar then dissects the cross, continues across and goes round another quarter to the right.

and circles the bars filling the centre of the circle as much as is required.

The fourth bar stops at the centre . . .

A few stitches are made at the centre before . .

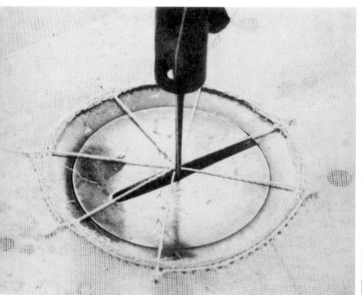

completing the fourth bar.

for the satin stitching round the edge.

The work is then turned at right angles in preparation . . .

This can be done in one or two rows depending on the weight of satin stitch required. It can also be padded with threads.

A line of straight stitching can be worked round the outside . . .

and a further decorative treatment added.

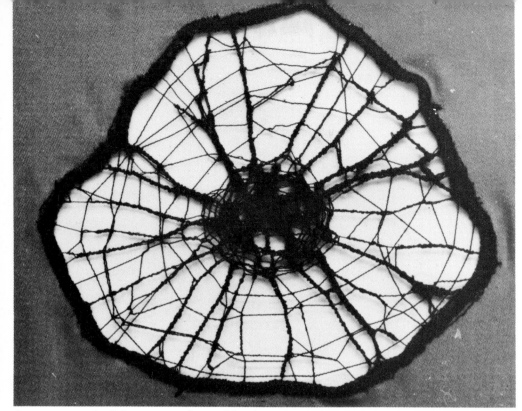

An assymetrical interpretation of basic cut-work has been used on cotton satin in black thread, some of the bars have been whipped with zigzag and the centre worked more openly.

*Goldsmiths' Dip AD*

Pulled and cut-work have been used together here, threads pulled together with a tight zigzag first and where more space was needed, threads cut away. Finally, stitched bars have filled certain areas with a dark lower and light upper thread.

*Goldsmiths' Judith Standeven*

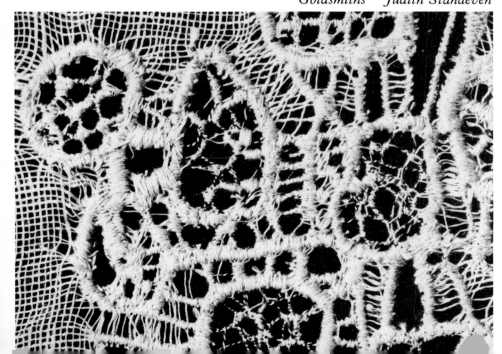

## Eyelets

The *Viking* domestic machine has two sized eyelet cover plates. A hole is punched with a stiletto in organdie . . .

The needle is positioned to the right and a straight stitch made. The needle throw bar is put to the medium setting and the fabric which has been placed in a frame is turned in an anti-clockwise direction. The threads can be cut or act as a padding to the satin stitch and with the larger spur a line of straight stitch first can also act as padding.

the hole forced over the spur and the lower thread is brought up.

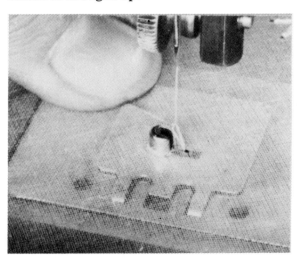

In the case of the larger spur a hole has to be cut in such a firm fabric as organdie but in a fine scrim the threads could be divided.

The sample shows both sizes of eyelet worked together as a texture, first with open zigzag which acted as a padding for close satin stitch.

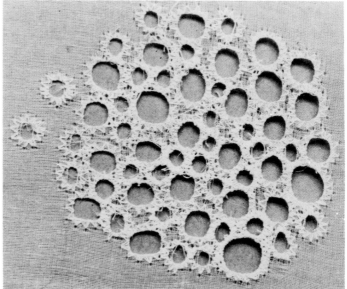

The same width throw has been used for both sizes of hole, in fact some holes have even been enlarged.

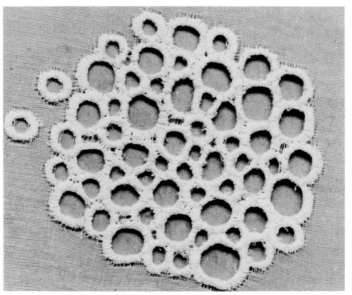

Eyelets worked on the *Irish* machine can produce a wider throw of stitching round the hole. These have been mounted with gold kid behind to shine through the holes.

*Judy Barry*

## Shifflei embroidery

This sample shows the multiple production of a pattern on the Shifflei machine. This is a manufacturing machine capable of reproducing metres (yards) of the same design. Small areas are first worked on different grounds with different threads. This design by Karen Nicol has been worked on

   (a)   orange velvet in gold metal thread
   (b)   grey felt in silver thread
   (c)   white cotton in white floss
   (d)   grey satin in tan cotton.

*Manchester   Karen Nicol*

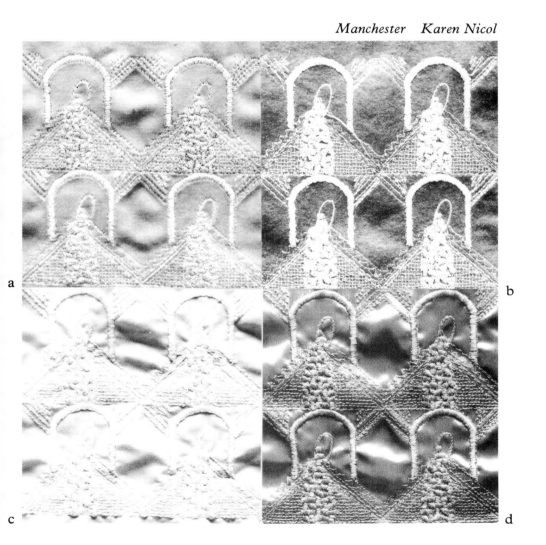

a

b

c

d

# 4 Designing for machine embroidery

## Working directly from natural objects

When sufficient confidence is felt with the machine it is possible to embroider directly from objects without hampering limitations of drawing and transferring the design to the fabric. By working in this way a full use will be made of the machine, instead of its being used as a means of tracing the drawing onto fabric and subsequently copying the drawn line in thread.

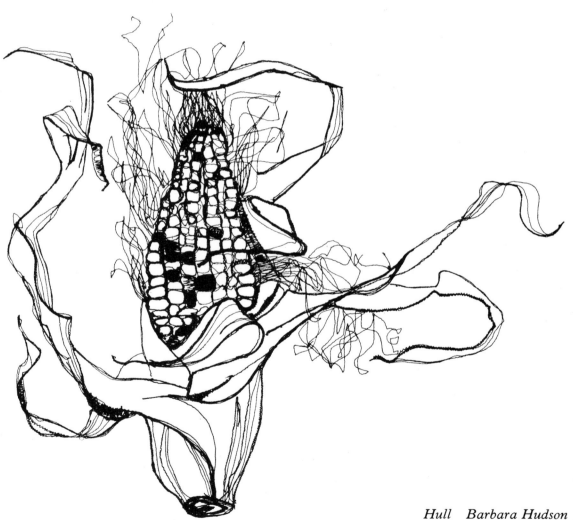

*Hull   Barbara Hudson*

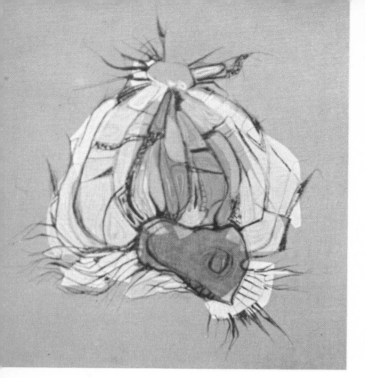

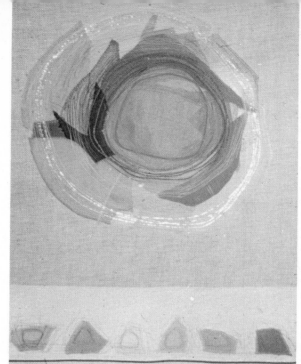

There should be no attempt to make a direct copy of a leaf or flower, but simplified basic lines should be sought as a means of studying the growth which is continually shaping the form of the plant. Instead of working from the outline of the leaf, a study should be made of its growth from the central vein, its direction and the twist which this gives the leaf, to the smaller veins which join it and the shapes which are formed between them.

◄ *Bulb* Silks and rayons applied to hessian ground with delineation in black thread worked on the Irish machine. Idea from the bottom of a crazed enamel bowl *Bristol Waterworks Company*

*Hedge* In the application of the shapes between the branches of the hedge, a low tonal range has been sought, enhanced by the use of reflective fabrics giving a greater variety of tone to their appearance

*Winter Sun* Silks, rayons and nets caught down with lurex and rayon threads in chain, straight stitch and zigzag on white lawn

Tufted hanging in two-ply rug wool, mercerised weaving threads and silk on hessian, the quality of colour has been gradated by the gradual inclusion of one colour or tone as another has been excluded.

PLATE 2

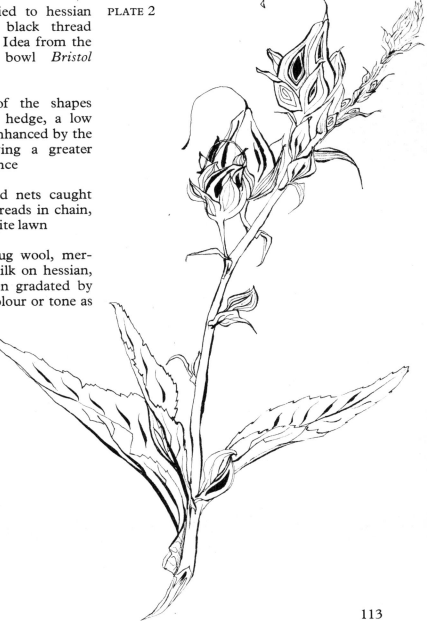

Most of the vein pattern will be visible on the underside of the leaf which should be studied from all sides not only the upper surface and in so doing it will be observed that the edge of the leaf results in the end of the growth.

In the same way it is important to learn how a flower is made up so that the working of petals is backed by the knowledge of their relation to the sepals and ovary, for all this decides the way in which the flower is set on the stalk and, once the growth is understood, the character of the flower can be more easily drawn.

A further understanding of the form would result if the flower were studied in all stages of its growth from the bud to the fruit and it might also be of benefit to make studies of these in order to see the change in shape of each successive part as it grows and diminishes in importance. This is particularly obvious in the rose where the sepals are of first importance in protecting the bud, curl back from the flower and finally form part of the tip of the fruit.

## Study of the plant

From this, progress can be made to a study of the plant; the way in which the leaves grow from the stem, either in pairs, alternately or in a spiral formation. A modified leaf, which originally protected the young bud, can be seen at the point where the flower grows from the main stem and both this and the swelling at the base of the stalk, where it joins the stem, should be considered. In many plants it is possible to use the root which not only completes it but adds interesting line and form that contrasts or conforms with other shapes in the plant.

It is often an advantage to work small plants two or three times their normal size, so that it is possible to select certain shapes which normally would be too small to work. Selection of line and form is of the utmost importance in designing directly from an object for the temptation is to use everything and this only leads to a confusion in the embroidery. In nature some things are more prominent than others and it is for the designer to decide whether these should be emphasized or whether there are other shapes which are of more importance to the design.

116

The plant itself often helps in this decision since certain lines or curves tend to be repeated and this repetition can be used to form a basis from which the rest of the design grows.

## Seed pods and fruit

A detailed study of the seed pod and fruit of various plants is worth considering. First the outer form from the attachment at the stem to, in the case of the apple, the sepals at its tip, including the markings on the skin which can be used in a decorative rather than a naturalistic way to emphasize the form. Then studies can be made from cut sections showing the pips and case in which they lie, the position of the sepals, the remains of the style running through the centre from this to the stalk and the fine line visible in the flesh of the apple, echoing the line of the seed case.

117

Not all fruits have their style and sepals at the tip, the poppy for example is formed above the flower so that only the sepals are visible at its base. This fruit makes a particularly decorative form of pattern when it is cut in various ways.

## Vegetables

Vegetables can also prove surprisingly decorative; the string of onions, for example, showing first the root hairs on the underside of the top ones, then the characteristic shapes of the middle ones and finally the leaves of the lower ones, forming a plait which links them all together. Parsnips worked in fine white thread on black net can show the main shape of the root drawn in crisp vigorous lines with the root hairs treated more tentatively. In making several studies of the same subject from different angles, an attempt should be made to relate them in order to form a composition in preparation for the arrangement of more dissimilar shapes.

A design can also be suggested by the vege-table on the still flowering plant as is seen in the herbal drawings of the sixteenth century where the whole cycle of the plant is shown.

It is not only exotic forms which inspire ideas; familiar fruit and vegetables prove as interesting and have greater decorative qualities than at first sight appear. Plant forms can be considered with fruit and vegetables when designing a group, for their use will add different shapes and textures which will complement the others. In an attempt to achieve pattern, as much attention should be given to the shapes between, as to the fruit and vegetables themselves. The aim should be not to set them realistically in containers which only cut up the form but to relate the basket or bowl to the forms it contains. In the same way any decoration on the container should be used to emphasize its shape rather than compete with the other forms by the strength of its pattern.

*Hull    Margaret Rackham*

## Asymmetrical and geometric qualities of natural forms

By incorporating cut sections with the whole form, greater play is given to the asymmetrical quality of fruit and vegetables, and here it is of more interest to retain the natural freedom of shape of the cut sections than to use a geometrical formula. An illustration of this is seen in lemons, where the naturally asymmetrical form of each section gives variety to their shape.

*Hull    Angela Jagger*

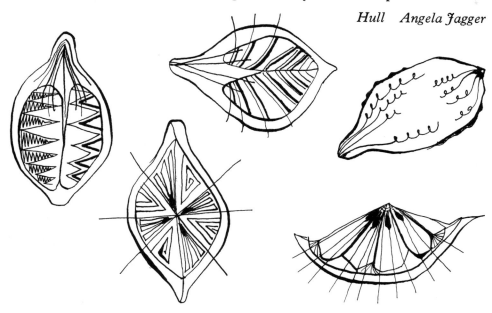

This does not preclude the adaptation of natural forms to a geometric structure, in fact nature itself is based on laws from which geometry has arisen and it is in divergence from these laws that asymmetrical qualities have developed. An instance of this is seen in the pea and its pod, both of which contain a circular form in their structure, the pod by prolonging the curve at its tip and the pea echoing this in its smaller radius. This does not always result in a perfect circle since the sides are sometimes flattened by the growth of the peas on either side. It is often better to use a geometric shape in a repetitive design rather than a natural form since repetition tends to diminish the spontaneity of a free shape but increases the decorative quality of a formal one. When grouping objects together, interest can be increased by the use of varieties in size as well as shape so that the delicacy of fine lines in stems and leaves contrasts well with the bold forms of fruit and vegetables. Nuts can also be included as they provide such varied shapes; open beech nuts forming intersecting triangles, the simple shape of sweet chestnuts against the complexity of the prickly case, the horsechestnut case which produces individual spines, hazel and cob nuts with outer leaves protecting the shell and walnuts which when opened along the spine show curly shapes formed by the nut, skin and shell.

121

## Non-figurative design

Some of these shapes if used together could be developed to form extremely interesting patterns, for all non-figurative design is based on form of some sort. It is quite hopeless to scribble certain lines in the hope that it will eventually turn into an 'abstract', all that will result is an indecision of form which no rearrangement of shapes will rectify, unless this is based on an idea containing form.

*Hull   Rae North*

Stages in this development are shown in the studies derived from a brussels sprout.

The first is a direct drawing from the cut sprout

the second prolongs certain curves in an attempt to find the rhythm of the design

and the third correlates the shapes formed by these lines by applying fabrics which increase, by their texture, the importance to the design of these shapes. This gradual development from the original shape to non-figurative form, presents unlimited possibilities, for although it may end by bearing little relationship, on the surface, to the original idea, the ground work is present as a positive factor from which the construction of the design is derived.

## Sources of inspiration

Art galleries and exhibitions of painting and constructional work should be visited in order to study the varied approaches which artists use to achieve their realization of form so that the outlook on the craft of embroidery is prevented from becoming narrow and completely divorced from other forms of art. Where possible some painting and three-dimensional work should be attempted if only to experience the feeling of working with such material, for the practice and use of these will result in a greater understanding of one's own medium and will influence and suggest other approaches to the craft.

## Fish

It is important when designing from creatures to understand their fundamental structure, or if this is impracticable, their movement and balance. In the case of the fish, use can be made of the backbone and head, for in a study of the way in which the vertebrae are articulated and joined to the head, a greater understanding of the form will result. The simplicity of curve in its body is echoed by the fins and tail and in the markings, whilst the curves produced have a great affinity with the movement of the frame and follow very naturally in machine embroidery.

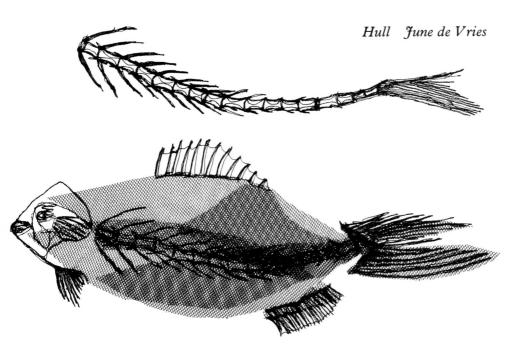

*Hull   June de Vries*

123

## Birds

The study of the carcass of a bird is rather more difficult but here use might be made of an X-ray photograph which will eliminate the form-concealing feathers. The placing of the head with relation to the rest of the body must be realized, the way in which the neck joins them and the positioning of the wings and legs, all of which are instrumental in the balance of the bird.

A study can then be made of the different feathers which are surprisingly varied in shape, ranging from soft, short breast feathers, firm blunt wing feathers to graceful curving tail feathers.

The pheasant's tail feather was worked directly on lawn with no. 50 machine embroidery cotton and here the direction of the quill was worked first and the barbs allowed to grow from it. These formed themselves into groups which it was thought better to emphasize rather than attempt to embroider each individual barb as this would have resulted in a great many parallel lines without increasing the form of the feather.

Once the form of the bird is understood it is possible to use the feathers to emphasize the shape, the curve of the wing and tail echoing the shape of the breast and the way in which the neck flows into the body. The decorative quality can then be derived from the markings and shape of the feathers and their relationship to the rest of the bird.

## Animals

The basic structure of animals can be seen rather more easily than that of birds and should play as important a part in their design as their decorative characteristics. The cat family for example offers many suggestions for design. The domestic cat is the easiest to study in its varied positions and lithe movements and many of these will provide graceful sweeping qualities for design.

The greater cats can be studied in zoos where their decorative features will be seen to advantage against the stark severity of their background. Care must be taken to use these sketches in a flat decorative manner and not too literally, for if they are transferred onto the material without this consideration, the general lines and form will be lost in an attempt at foreshortening.

The sketch should only be used as a starting point for the design and referred to for the characteristics of the animal, so that if ribs are shown beneath the skin in the sketch, these could be treated in a more emphatic and decorative manner in the design.

If the markings are numerous these can be made fewer and more important, while manes and tails can be simplified to suggest an outline or treated in detail so that fine lines are used to suggest hair. If it is necessary to divide the animal into sections in which to work decorative patterns it is best to do this anatomically, so that the head is shown clearly against the neck, which joins it to the body and the joints of the hind and fore legs make another natural division which can be used in a similar way.

## The human figure

Perhaps the most fascinating of all subjects is the human figure which is not only beautiful in its own right but lends itself to drapery and decorative treatment of clothing. A groundwork of life-drawing is essential so that there is a full understanding of the figure before it is drawn clothed, for if this is attempted without comprehension of the form beneath, the design is likely to result in a bundle of clothes with arms, legs and head emerging from it.

When working from a clothed figure it is important to realize the position of the limbs and trunk under the drapery and is necessary indicate these in the design

*Margaret Traherne*
*Victoria and Albert Museum*
*Crown Copyright*

129

for it is often possible to see the legs in a seated figure as well as the thorax with their relation to the hips. These lines will help in determining the areas of decoration on the garment or can be used to give greater emphasis to the form. If the design is transferred to the fabric, only the fundamental lines should be traced, so that when the tissue paper is removed these act as a general guide from which to work. If, when the embroidery is started, some of these lines are found to be wrong, as many fresh lines as are necessary should be stitched to correct this, it is after all of more importance to arrive at the right line through several attempts, than to leave the first line approximating to the one required. The figure can also be studied in the earliest forms

*Hull*
*Norma Wallis*

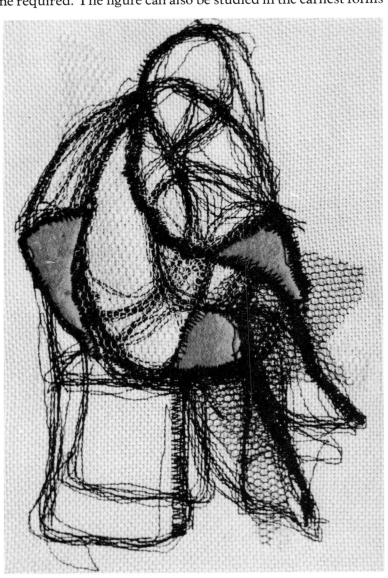

130

of art and has been depicted in paint, stone, stained glass, ceramics, metal, woven and printed textiles, wood, bone and many other materials, so there is great scope for study of objects in museums as well as books. As much attention should be given to this as the live figure when considering it as a form of decoration, and consideration should also be given to grouping of figures.

## Figure on a couch

Here the figure and the couch have been reduced to absolute essentials, producing a very dramatic yet simple quality to the design.

*Andrey Tucker*

## Mechanical forms

Mechanical objects provide very varied shapes from which to work. Clocks, the inside of typewriters, tills and machines of all kinds lend themselves to the curves and spirals which are such an integral part of machine embroidery.

If there is a wish to develop this further, many of these shapes will form a basis for non-figurative pattern.

*Hull*
*Nigel*
*Standerline*

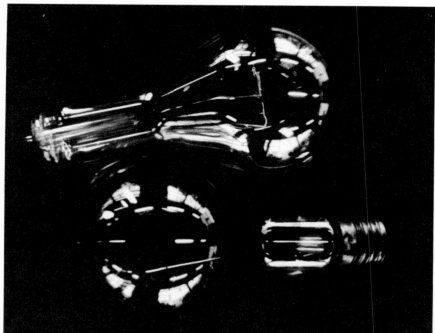

*Hull*
*Martin Lord*

132

The interest of the embroiderer in the spinning wheel, was the relation of the wheel itself to the rest of the construction, lines of which were carried through until triangular and rectangular shapes were found, drawn boldly and emphasized with net.

*Hull    Norma Wallis*

## Architectural form

Architectural design will also provide interesting features for study, particularly where the construction is visible, as in towers, bridges and piers.

The use of actual buildings should be treated with a little more care as the temptation may be to use too many details and so confuse the design.

Wrought iron can also suggest various curved and linear forms for which machine line has an affinity.

## Inanimate objects

Many inanimate objects prove decorative for design. Among these are shells which, however complex in shape, should be reduced to a basically simple form.

Those which have become eroded by the sea generally retain their mid-rib, from which the spiral formation grows, and it will help in an understanding of the whole form if such shapes are studied first. In this way the construction of the shell can be built into the design, and by using different shells together an inter-relation of shape will result. Interesting shapes and texture are also obtainable from stones.

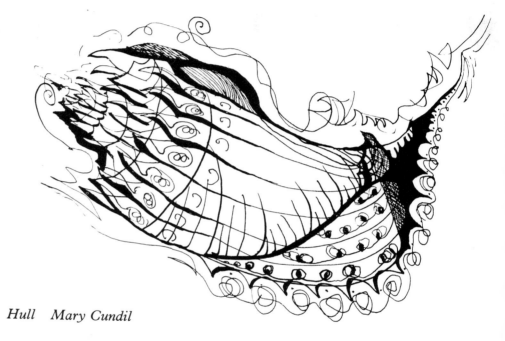

*Hull   Mary Cundil*

## Grouping of objects and use of perspective

When there is a need to group objects, particularly in panels and hangings, a background link of some kind may be the answer. Background is perhaps a misleading term which suggests the recession of planes. The use of this form of perspective in design can defeat the meaning of the term 'design' which is primarily concerned with the interpretation of ideas into pattern.

This means that the background is used, either in close connection with the objects, as is suggested by the photograph of caged birds, to form part of the pattern but not to dominate it, or is implied...

136

as *Girls Washing Their Hair* illustrates. Here use has been made of bowls and towels but not of the place in which they are.

*Hull    June de Vries*

With modification, a decorative use can be made of perspective of what we recognise as distance in a photograph. It is worth considering the treatment of distance and perspective in early art forms, where objects further away were reduced in size and placed higher than those in the foreground, so forming decorative bands of pattern.

The designer should be looking for pattern and form in everything; from the minute examination of wood grain, to the full growth of a tree . . .

and the way it has been trained to grow. It may also be sought in unlikely places, from the attraction of iron filings for a magnet in science to mathematical formulae in linear form, so that not only is the designer developing ideas which have been used before but pattern is recognised in other fields than art and is interpreted for use in machine embroidery.

# 5 The influence of the background weave on embroidery

## Influence of fabric on the machine line

The quality of fabric plays an important part in the design of machine embroidery since it has such an influence on the line made by the machine. Not only does this line vary in appearance on the same fabric when the tension is altered, but using the same tension it will vary on different types of fabric. The variation in appearance of fabrics is not only due to the different yarns used in their manufacture but also to the variation in the weave, so that a woollen cloth looks different from a cotton even when woven in the same way, and the same yarn woven in various ways gives a totally different appearance to the cloth. Although this is an elementary observation, it is made in order to encourage the embroiderer to use more than plainly woven cotton and silks as background fabrics, so that not only should one be aware that an even tension on lawn gives a smooth line and that on net the same line has an uneven appearance where the two threads twist round one another between the mesh but also one should be conscious of what happens to the tension and thread on an elastic fabric, such as wool, or to the stitch if a silk ground is chosen. Not only does the texture of the fabric have an influence on the line but its tone with relation to that of the thread will also affect the look of the stitch. A white line on black cloth looks more spiky than a black line on white, while a stitch which is close in tone to the fabric on which it is worked gives a richer effect than one which is very much deeper or paler. The background to some extent determines the method of machine embroidery as well as influencing the choice of design, because a heavy treatment for coarse fabrics demands a bolder design than one on net or organdie, which from a practical point of view needs a light treatment. This does not, of course, prevent rich, heavy treatments on fine fabrics and light ones on coarse grounds.

A very different appearance is given to the moss stitch in floss thread on the felt and moygashel background. On the felt where no weave is competing in a textural way, the full richness of the stitch can be appreciated, but on the coarsely woven ground the loops are almost lost and only their sheen and colour help to distinguish them from the ground.

*Judy Barry*

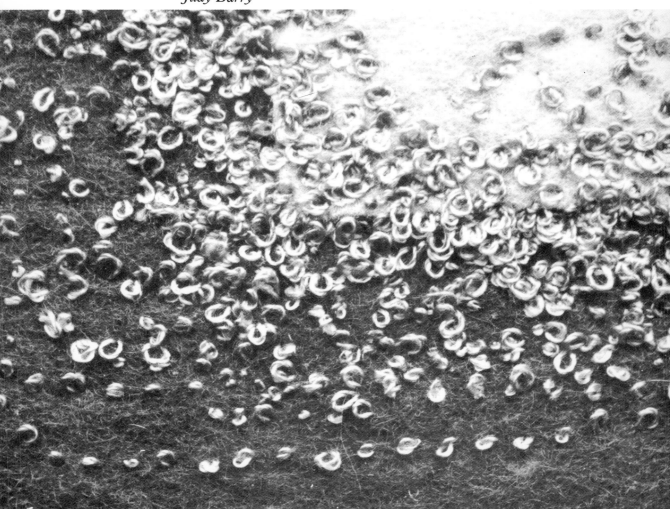

*Judy Barry*

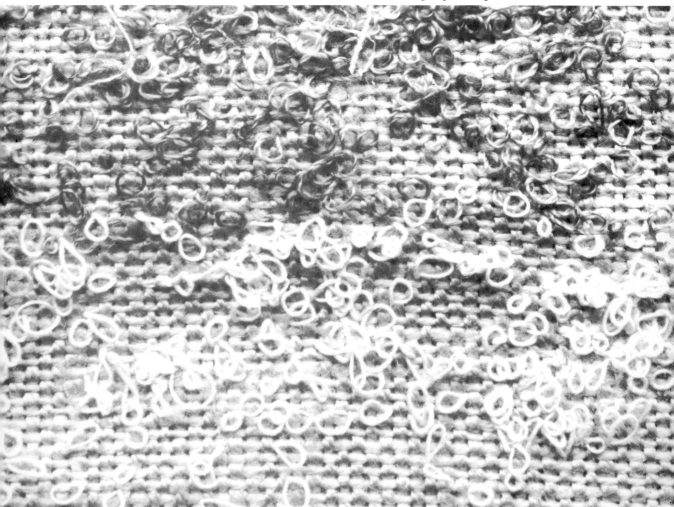

## Transparent fabrics

Muslin not only allows threads at the back to be visible from the front but retains holes made by the needle and held by the tight tension.

The line on dress net can vary considerably since one is particularly conscious of the twist of the upper and lower threads between the holes of the mesh, a tight even tension giving a straight line, a normal even tension giving a slightly twisted line and an uneven tension giving a blurred line.

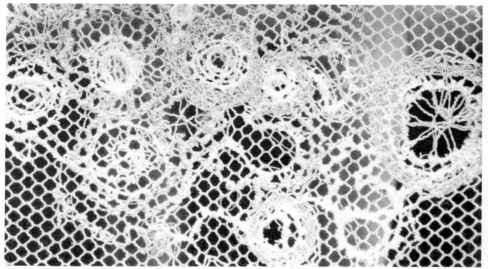

Design almost ignoring the fabric except as a contrast between heavy stitching and light net is concerned.

*Hull    Wendy Shearman*

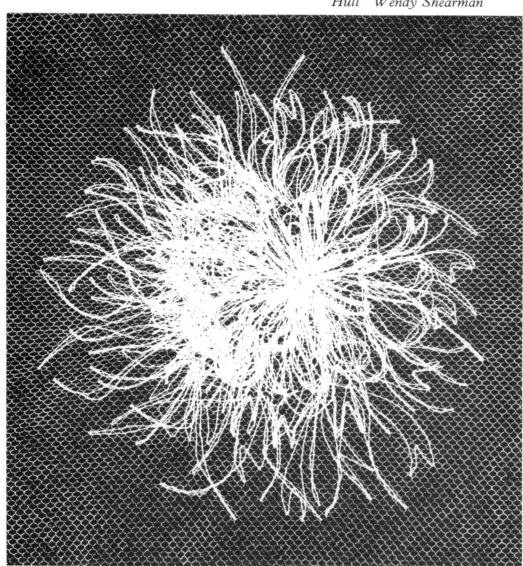

◄ *Goldsmiths'    Judith Standeven*

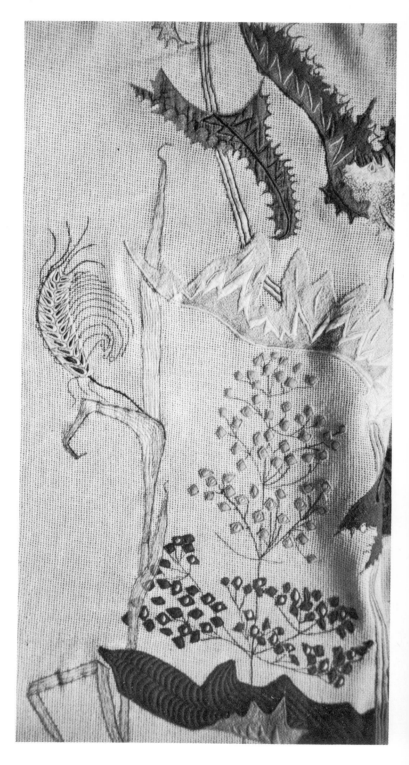

*Hull   Wendy Shearman*

144

A coarser open mesh fabric is dishcloth, woven in soft cotton in a gauze weave. Care must be taken to stretch this cloth evenly in the frame, especially if other fabrics are to be applied to it. This fabric gives a lively appearance against the matt qualities of the felt and organdie applied to it and it is interesting to notice the quilted quality of the unstitched felt on the leaf.

Hessian and linen scrims are so loosely woven that as long as the needle throw can gather them in, great width of weave can be bound by the tight zigzag tension into relatively narrow bands of stitching where this is required.

*Goldsmiths' Judith Standeven*

Broader bands are achieved by repeated zigzagging with a normal tension. The quality given by the machine twist is very different from that of the lurex plate in the previous example.

*Goldsmiths'  Frances Challis*

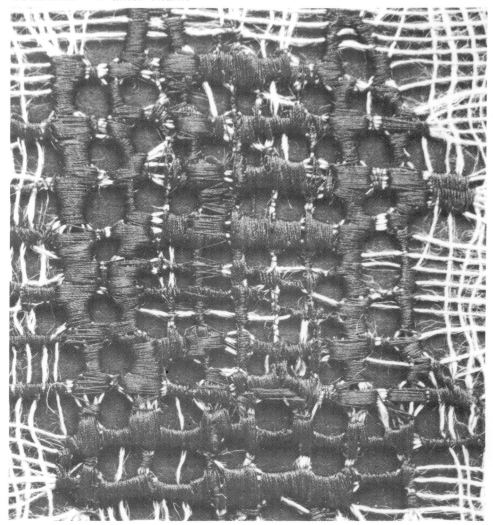

Here threads have either been pulled or cut away from parts of the design. In the upper one only the warp threads have been over-cast whilst the weft threads have been removed. These have been linked with machine thread bars in two tones of thread. The stitching of the lower is very heavy in comparison with the ground fabric and achieves a very rich appearance.

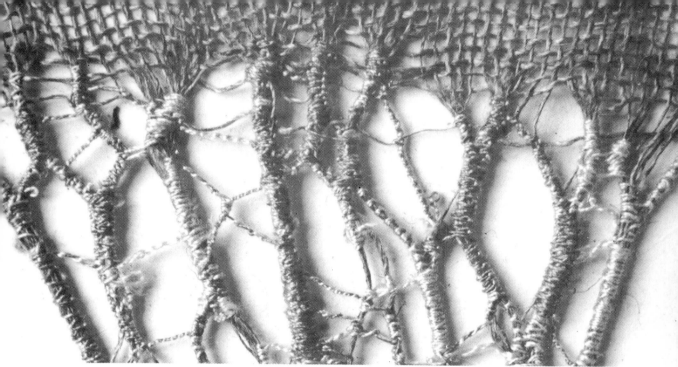

*Goldsmiths'   Judith Standeven*

*Goldsmiths'   Anne Vaughan*

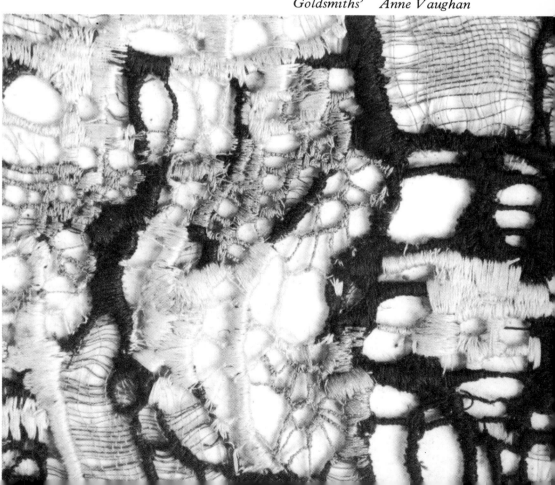

This flower head has been worked in a thread very much coarser than the black gauze on which it is worked, this has then been stretched over a lurex fabric which glints through, giving the impression that the embroidery is held in space.

*Audrey Tucker*

This beginner's sample makes it possible to see the different methods so far discussed in the same piece of work.

*Goldsmiths'    Judith Standeven*

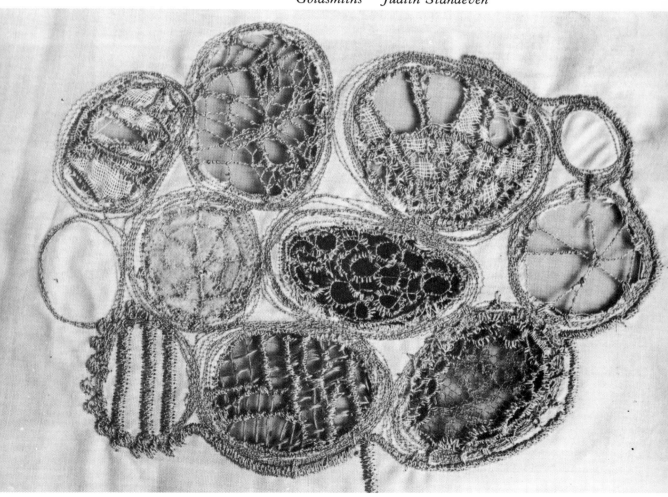

## Plain, twill and slub weaves

The machine embroidery thread lying on the surface of this fine silk fabric is simple in comparison to the complex texture of the ground. This is due to light reflecting from the warp and weft threads with a strong contrast in tone. The mercerized thread does not have such a high degree of reflection.

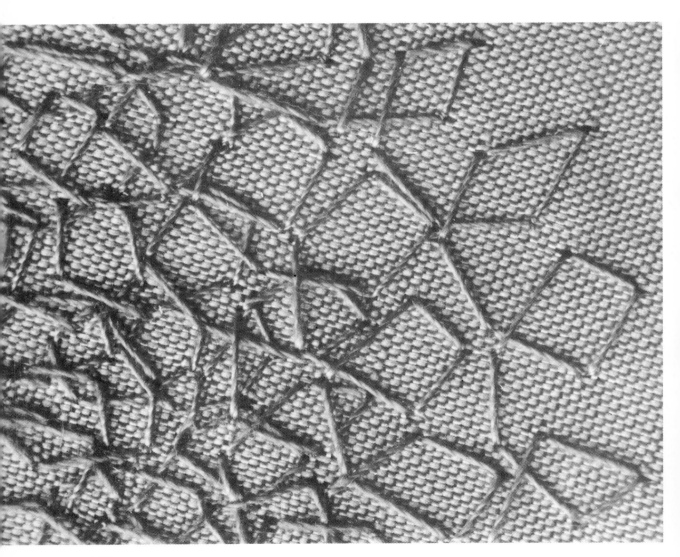

A satin weave also has a highly reflective quality and gives a smooth richness to the ground in strong contrast to the texture of the chain and moss stitch.

*Judy Barry*

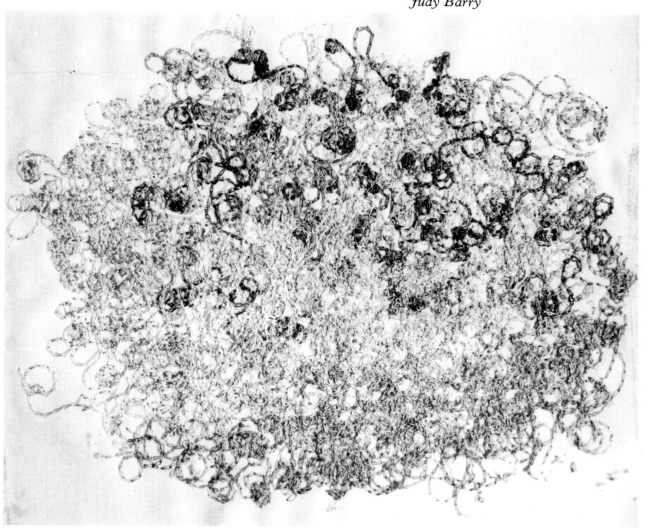

The plain weave of this cotton cloth provides a matt background for the floss and mercerized threads of this panel and increases the three dimensional quality of the stitching. The glint on the threads of this mercerized ground provides a lightly textured ground for the bold stitching.

*Judy Barry*

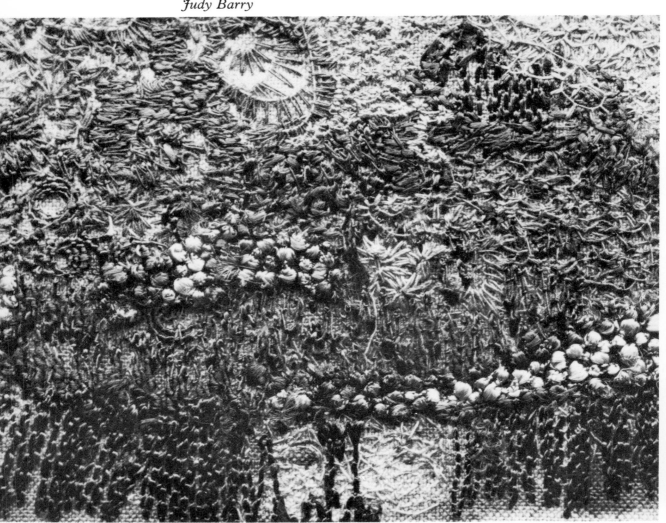

The twill is a distinctive diagonal weave which is still apparent through the applied chiffons. The grouping at the edge of the satin stitch can be seen in the troughs of the weave.

*Audrey Tucker*

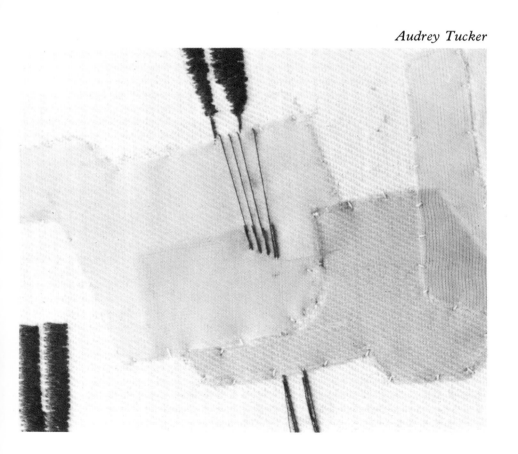

The stitch line has been kept fairly straight on this ribbed silk by the use of a tight top tension, but on the slub fabric the looser tension allows the straight stitch to disappear producing a chalky texture to the line. The narrower bands of satin stitch are affected by the slub and produce a break in the line but the heavier bands which have been stitched several times are not so affected.

*Hull    Hillary Bremner* ▶

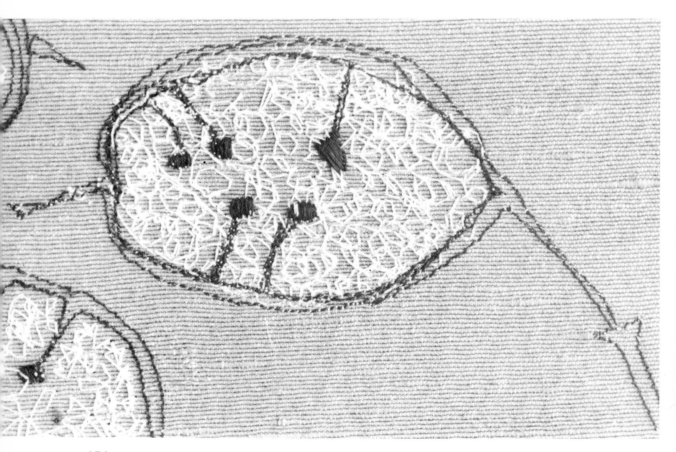

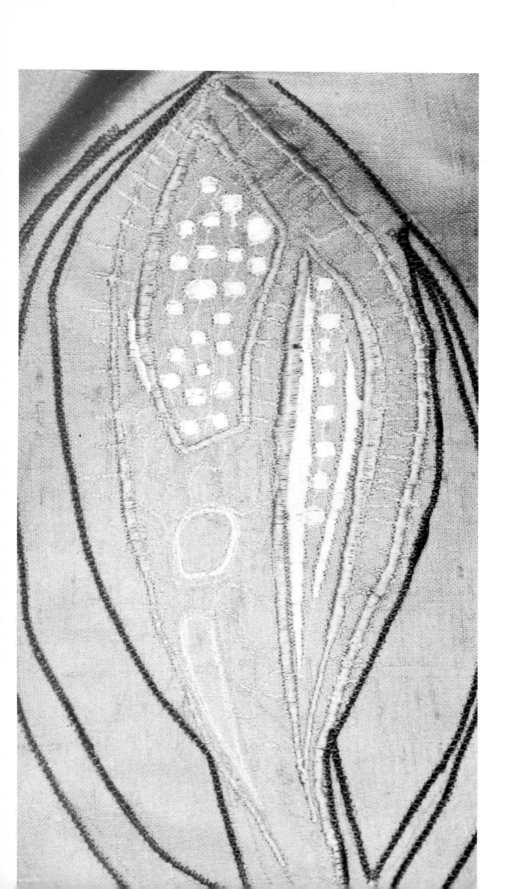

In this part of a stole, the slub silk background has been textured with stitches leaving the letters in plain fabric, the main words only being outlined in gold thread. Picking up the spool thread and running with the weave of the cloth had produced a rich exciting ground leaving the simplicity of the lettering to be read easily from a distance.

*Judy Barry*

In this example from a child's tunic, both the warp and weft threads are slubbed giving an interesting unevenness to the black stitched line allowing flecks of light ground to show between the double lines at times.

*Gay Swift*

The same stitch worked on three different backgrounds gives the stitch a different appearance, direct and firm on the hessian and net, softer with a quilted appearance on the silk and almost disappearing on the silk and net.

*Hull    Norma Wallis*

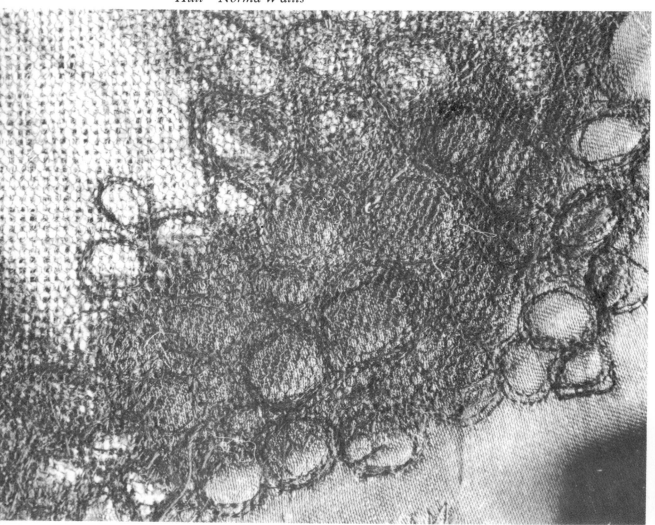

## Tufted fabrics

Towelling provides a pile background, some being denser than others, so that in those cases single lines of stitching are often covered by the loops of the pile and have to be strengthened with several lines. In this example the pile is not so long so that single lines are visible, but the use of a number of straight lines combined with applied fabrics produces an interesting contrast with the irregular background.

*Goldsmiths'   Judith Standeven*

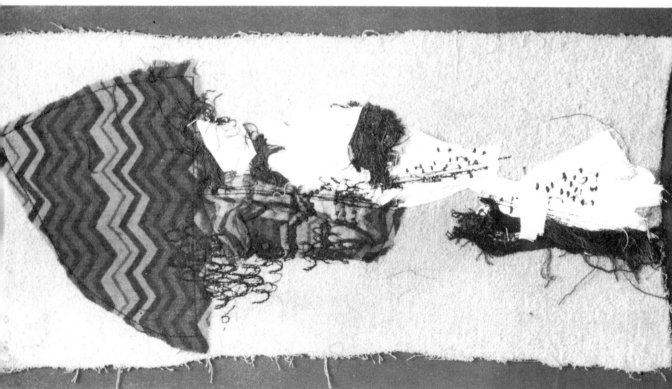

In the shorter pile of a close velvet, fine stitches disappear giving a quilted effect where they stitch the pile down.

*Manchester    Geraldine Keating*

On the long piled plush the direction in which the pile lies has been altered by the stitching and the pile has veiled the stitching, partially hiding it.

*Gay Swift*

## PVC surfaces

These vary in weight and type, some being bonded onto a cloth ground others being transparent. It is possible with the bonded ones to stitch fairly closely but if they are not reinforced the PVC is cut by the needle holes set close together. In this example of pattern darning, the PVC is very heavy and the stitches are close together.

*Manchester    Geraldine Keating*

On the transparent PVC the satin stitch has been worked fairly openly and where more solid areas were required more stitches were worked over the same area. The tension has distorted the ground so that the light catches it very strongly.

*Goldsmiths'    Judith Standeven*

## Woven stripes

The stripe in the ground has been tucked and pleated with zigzagging and couched threads to produce a wave-like quality to the design. The manipulation of the fabric has been the main source of inspiration behind this design.

*Becky Mullins*

## Embroidered grounds

In this detail of a burse the background has been worked on the satin twill ground to produce a more lively background for the applied torch, moon and cross. The movement round the circle is particularly interesting and draws the eye to that area giving it movement and life which a plainly woven cloth would be unable to do.

*Judy Barry*

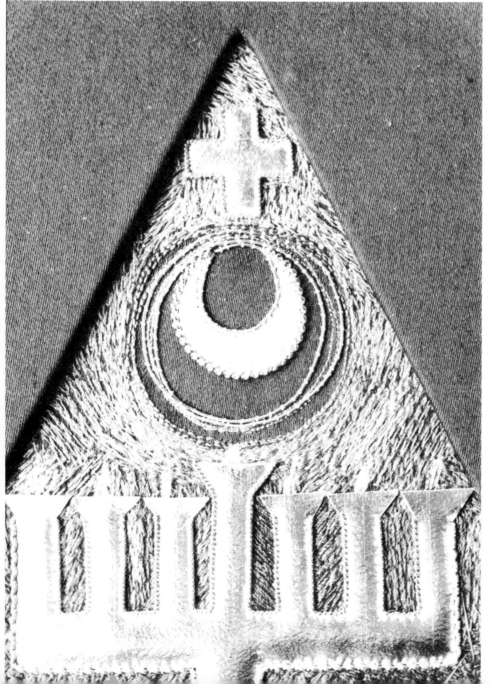

# 6 Applied fabrics

## Tone and texture of applied fabrics

After experimenting with stitches in relation to the background, it is possible to introduce other fabrics by applying them to the ground in order to use them for additional colour and texture. It is worth considering the great variety in tone of different white cloths and by applying matt and shiny fabrics to a transparent net or organdie ground, to build up a composition based entirely on texture. The embroidery stitch will have as much influence as the applied fabrics since it not only adds further texture but can be used to link areas of fabric into a coherent pattern. Tone and texture are so closely linked that it is impossible to use one without finding the other present; some white fabrics are of necessity more cream or blue than others, either because they can be bleached no whiter as in the case of wool, or they appear deeper in tone because of their structure, as do velvets and brocades.

This variety is carried further when different fabrics of the same colour are used together and it is interesting to notice the influence which light has on their appearance. Shot silks, brocades, satins and velvets are all affected by the way in which the light falls on them so that they can be placed in various directions in one piece of work to make the maximum use of this quality. This reduces the necessity for a great many fabrics, at least to begin with and forms an important link in the continuity of the design.

*Hull    Susan Deighton*

166

## Relation of background to applied fabrics

The best way to begin designing with applied fabrics is to use them for their own sake, allowing them to suggest ideas for design and to augment the textures given by the machine. Fabrics can be cut roughly with straight and curved edges, varying in size and shape as the design demands and being restricted to two colours in as many shades as is necessary. The background can play an important part in the design, if the majority of fabrics to be applied have a lustre, a woollen background with a well defined weave would enhance this, if a ground with a rich sheen is used then fabrics of rather rougher texture show to advantage.

An alternative is to attach various fabrics to a backing of lawn or calico, depending on their weight, so that they themselves make a composite fabric. The shapes which are made by the cut edges of the fabric should suggest a design which can then be taken further by the machine, and this will act as a means of sewing down the edges of the fabric as well as developing the design.

*Hull    Rhona Catchpole*

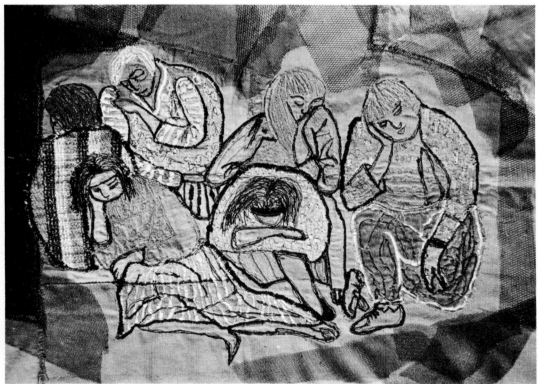

## Methods of applying fabrics

There are various methods for sewing fabrics down. The simplest is to tack them in position on the background fabric or backing (which will not show) and then stitch them either on a straight-stitch or swing-needle machine with the feed teeth up and the foot holding the fabrics in position. On the straight-stitch machine, the stitch should be small to medium and it may be necessary to work round the edges of some fabrics more than twice but the swing-needle should be set with a medium to large bite depending on the thickness of the cloth and making an open zigzag once round the edge of the fabric. This prevents any puckering and makes the planes of the two fabrics level so that they appear as one, and the worker is not over conscious of where one fabric stops and another begins.

## Development of the lines of the design

This makes it possible to ignore or develop the lines stitching the applied fabrics, especially if they have been varied in width, so that shapes can be linked and built up by the use of straight or satin stitching which will vary in weight according to the importance of the line or necessity for a firm stitch to hold the fabric in place. A good deal of thought must therefore be given to the placing of fabrics which are loosely woven or made from yarns which fray easily as the heavy stitching of these may result in putting the design out of balance. Another advantage of stitching the fabrics down in this way is that, being to a certain extent unaware of the stitched edge, it enables a continuous line to be stitched across different textures which results in variations in its appearance.

Having built up the form of the design first with fabrics and then clarified it with line, it is possible to develop certain areas further by the use of pattern with stitching either on the shapes themselves or, if these are to remain simple, in the background in order to emphasize the simplicity of these shapes more clearly.

*Bradford    Bernadette O'Donnell*

### Application of shapes roughly corresponding to those of the design

Another method, where the original design plays a greater part, is to take a tracing of the design on tissue paper and then cut fabrics to be applied, fairly roughly following shapes in the design. The tissue paper is put over the fabrics in order to help when placing them for tacking. This is temporarily removed whilst stitching them to the backing with the presser foot and, finally, the tracing is tacked down on top of the applied fabrics and stitched with the darning foot or in the frame. Many of the newly stitched lines do not coincide with the edges of the fabric since these were only cut roughly and this will add a fluid quality to the design. If it would improve certain parts of the work, after the tissue paper has been torn away, some fabrics can be cut back to the edge of the designed line and stitched again. It is then possible to build up the embroidery directly from the fabrics, using the edges and shapes and modifying the lines obtained from the tracing so that the two fuse together to suggest more spontaneous forms than is possible by the minute copying of the original design.

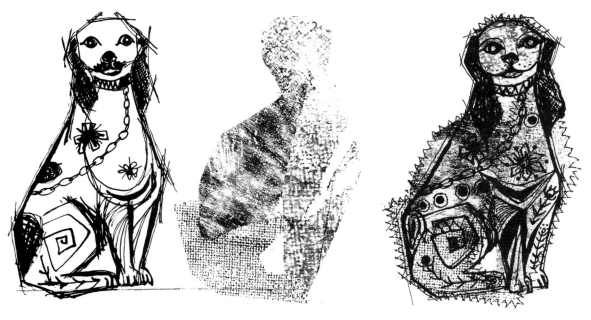

The seated figure was worked in this way and the cutting of the shapes was of equal importance as the lines of the design, which they echo. The simplicity of these shapes was maintained in the embroidery; the line and form being emphasized to the exclusion of decoration.

170

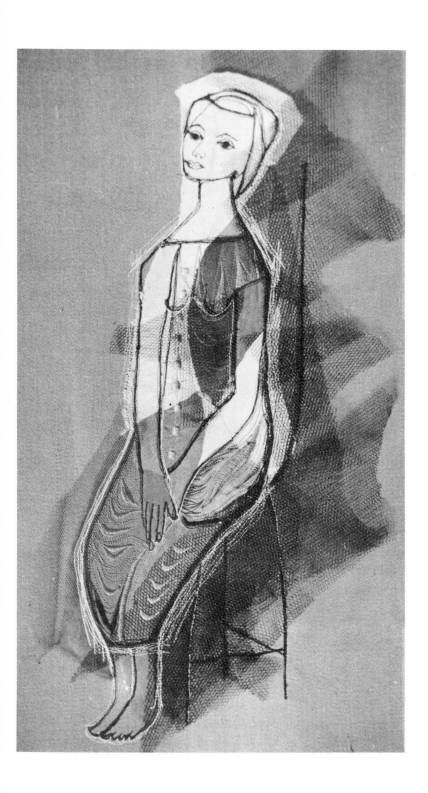

## The use of the stitched lines of the design in applying fabrics

If a closer interpretation of the design is needed, the main lines can be stitched through the tissue paper tracing. A piece of fabric, larger than the area to which it is going to be applied, is tacked in position to the ground. The work is then reversed, placed in a frame and stitched along the traced line for that particular shape. Turning it back to the right side, the fabric is cut close to the stitched line before the next piece of fabric is applied in the same way. There is a temptation with this method to apply those areas which are most prominent and then deal with those which are not so easily seen, but by breaking the design down it will be possible to see the lower layers which should be stitched first and realize those areas which should be applied afterwards. To give a simple example, the body of a bird should be applied before its wing. When the fabrics have been applied in this way, it is necessary to stitch two or three times over the raw edges left when they were cut and if one of these lines of stitching is taken onto the background this will merge the two fabrics together.

It is also possible to emphasize further those lines which are of most importance to the design, by working more than three lines of straight stitching on the edge of the upper fabric.

*Gay Swift*

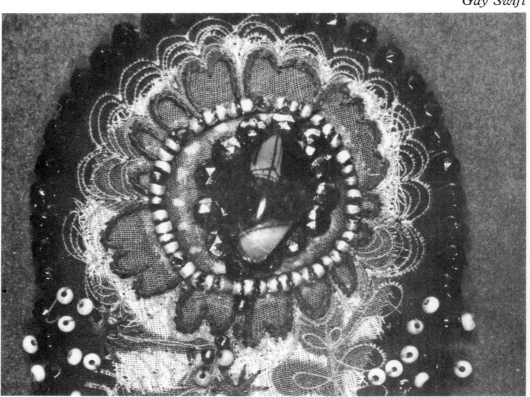

If the edges are stitched with a swing-needle machine it is as well to work a line of open zigzag; this is quite sufficient to stop fabrics from fraying and it softens the edge, the line can always be made stronger by the use of close satin stitch.

*Manchester    Ron Warde*

## Automatically stitching fabrics down with a satin stitch edge

When simple areas of material are applied on their own with no overlapping to a heavy background, it is advisable to cut them to the size and shape required and sew them down with the presser foot, preferably with a zigzag stitch; this will prevent any puckering and will prove satisfactory if the article is to be laundered frequently. When light fabrics are applied to fine grounds such as net or organdie, care should be taken that both fabrics are evenly stretched before stitching in a frame. In any case fabrics should always be tacked down when they are under no strain so that they can be stretched together ready for embroidery, for if fabrics are stitched to a pliable ground, which is already taut, they will be unable to stretch as much and when the work is removed from the frame, the applied materials will become wrinkled.

## Use of colour

Coloured fabrics are greatly influenced by their own texture and when placed next to each other, become altered in both colour and tone, because they appear to contrast more with each other when they are close together than they do when seen apart. This is why a great many colours of the same tone, seen together appear very dazzling, each being affected by the ones surrounding it. This is not so apparent when the colours are varied in tone as they are not equally dominant but even so, such a quantity becomes tiring to look at because of the insistence of the colour and the eye is unable to rest on any part of the design to consider the line and form. It is worth putting a limitation on the choice of colours for each piece of work, whilst using as many tones of these as is advisable and adding a little of other colours if it is found to be necessary. Since the choice of fabrics for appliqué is so wide and they are so different in appearance, a sufficiently wide range of tones will be found.

It is essential to collect a variety of fabrics for this puspose, either from dressmaking, but here care must be taken in the selection of patterned materials since they are often difficult to use, or by buying small quantities of any fabrics which may prove suitable. Those coloured fabrics which are to be used should be placed against the background in order to see the effect of this upon them as well as each other. This sometimes means the sacrifice of one or more colours, which attractive in themselves, produce discord when used with others. If one of these colours is particularly fascinating the rest can be eliminated and fresh colours and background chosen which will enhance it; other tones of this colour can be used as well as a secondary colour which incorporates some of the first in its make-up. If a rich hyacinth blue is the focal point, other shades of slightly different blues may help with several tones of olive green to complement the main colour, and if the main colour is a secondary one, such as orange, then it is possible to use tones on both the red and yellow side of the scale and it may not be necessary then to introduce any other colours.

## Effects achieved by the use of nets

The colour can also be affected by placing over each other transparent fabrics such as dress net and, to a certain extent, fine organdie, organzas and chiffons, if these are not too opaque. Variations in tones of one colour can be attempted entirely in nets applied to a ground of the same colour in a mid or dark tone. There is the possibility of using both light and dark nets on the middle tone fabric but only nets lighter in tone on the darker; this often gives a glowing effect and can be an exciting way in which to work. Different effects are obtained by the use of more than one layer of net; if a very light tone is needed it may take three or four layers before the background ceases to interfere.

In some cases the way in which these overlay one another produces a definite pattern and in allowing nets of different tone to overlap, a third tone will be formed.

## Suggestion of shapes given by the overlapping of nets

Further possibilities can be achieved by the use of different colours and here not only the tone but the colour of the background will affect the nets. By laying them over and under each other, changes of colour as well as tone will be seen, and by cutting various shapes and laying them on the background, the character given by the overlapping of curved or straight edges may suggest fish, boats, trees, figures or buildings as ideas for design.

The overlapping of two nets gives three possible lines to follow, those made by the edges of both pieces of net and the shape which is formed by them. Generally the edge made by the top net is the most distinct, especially when a light net overlaps a dark or this is reversed and it is not always necessary to emphasize it with a line as it is with that of the under net. If a medium tone is used over light or dark net, the shape formed by the two together is visible but this will not be so obvious if more than one layer of the top net is used. As there is no fear of net fraying it does not have to be stitched, unless the design demands a greater strength than the edge of the net can give or the embroidery is intended for an article which has to be washed frequently, in which case the edges can be sewn down with machine embroidery cotton the colour of the net or background, whichever is the least visible.

PLATE 3   *Eclipse*   A variety of furnishing fabrics and linings have been applied to a ▶ book muslin ground, entirely covering it. Net, silks and black buckram have then been applied for the sun, lines of light thread increase the spinning movement as they flicker through and on top of the black net
*Senior Commonroom, University of York*

*Vibrations*   A panel worked entirely in free satin stitch on a closely woven blue cotton ground. The frame was moved with the left hand, the right hand continually operating the stitch width lever. The top tension was slightly lighter than the bottom tension throughout to give the satin stitch different coloured edges   *Joy Clucas*

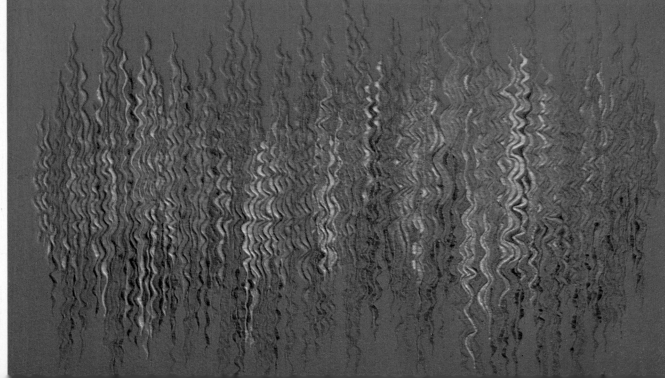

## Use of net with relation to other fabrics

The fluid quality given by nets alone can be destroyed by the introduction of other fabrics; this may be partly due to the fact that they are too heavy but is also likely to be because they were not considered with the nets and background in the first place and have only been added as an afterthought. Such fabrics by their weight tend to overbalance the sensitive relationship between the colour and texture of the nets and do not provide anything to compensate for this.

If the design is based from the beginning on the use of a variety of textures, it is possible to continue adding to these with different fabrics including net which is often of the greatest help in softening contours and partially altering colour and tone.

*Hull    Norma Wallis*

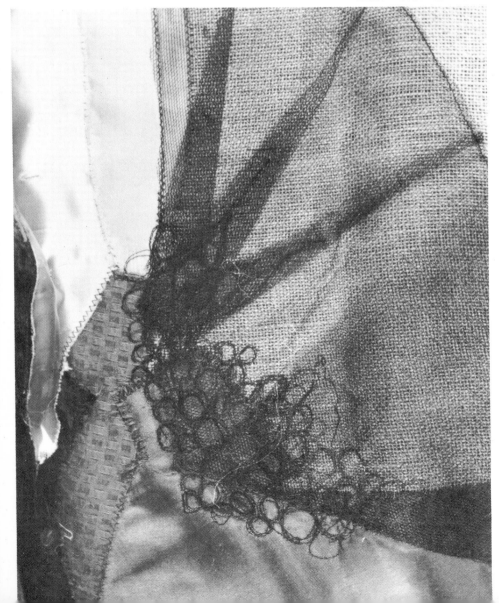

Another means of enriching the colour of applied fabrics is by couching yarns and threads over parts of them in order to add a three-dimensional quality as well as further texture. This quality is captured by the additional use of beads with the net and veiling.

*Gay Swift*

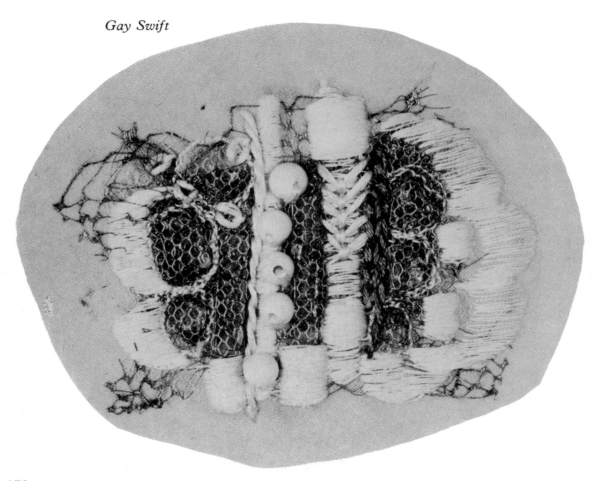

## Turned edges

In this piece of work in order to off-set the smooth felt and 'pebbley' wool, grounds have been machine embroidered with the *Irish* and Chain-stitch machines. The edges have been turned under to avoid the problem of fraying and to give a definite edge to each texture as well as a feeling of relief.

*Manchester    Helen Lord*

## Three dimensional surfaces

Hairy cloths such as teased wool, fur fabric and pile fabrics all give their own three dimensional quality to the surface

*Goldsmiths'   Judith Standeven*

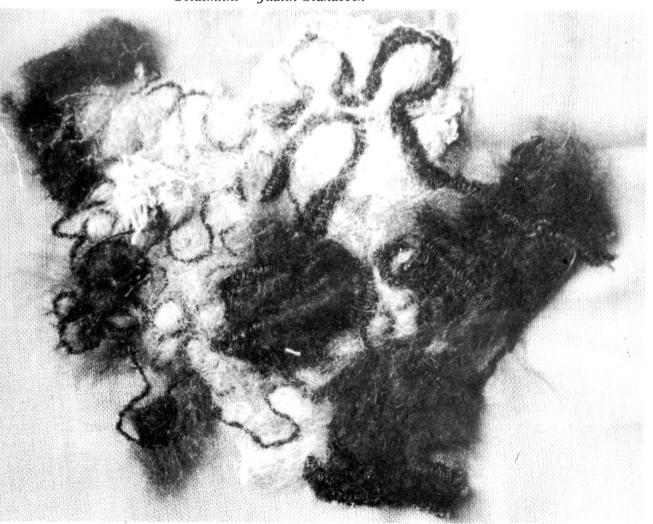

but more dramatic textures can be made with yarns looped to give a long pile. These yarns of different colour have been looped and twisted by hand and then straight stitched in position.

*Manchester    Julie Graham Rogers*

In this panel groups of *Cornelli* wool have been covered by printed voile and stitched between the bundles. An interesting use has been made of the other printed fabric to increase the three dimensional appearance of the work, by echoing spots and flowers in embroidery.

*Manchester    Julie Jeffries*

In this detail of a burse, the background fabric has been pleated and ribbon and knitted fabrics have been rolled and stitched to give as much relief as the gold cords.

*Judy Barry*

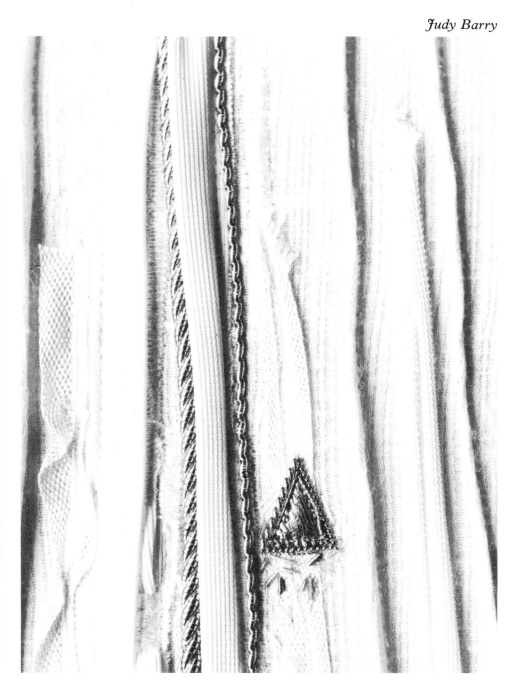

In this panel the main applied area has been worked in moss stitch eyelets and tacking, entirely covering the ground. The edge has been turned under but the tufted threads soften the edge and increase the three dimensional feeling which the form of the hill gives.

*Manchester    Susan Susksy*

# 7  Dyed and fabric printed grounds

## Tie and dye

Tie and dye is based on the resistance to the dyestuff by constricting the cloth. Fine cotton can be pleated with an iron to obtain a crisp edge and bound for 6 mm or 12 mm ($\frac{1}{4}$ in. or $\frac{1}{2}$ in.) with string, at various intervals, or gathered up in bunches, bound and tied tightly to prevent dye creeping in. The position and size of light areas can be roughly planned before tying and is controlled, in the pleated method, by the difficulty of constricting too wide a pleat. Close or open binding can be used, with the end of the string slipped through the last few rows of this.

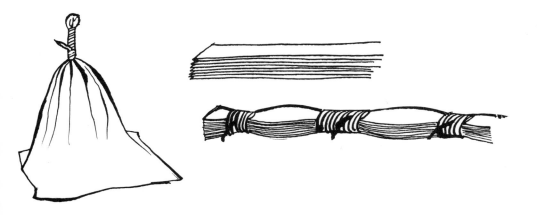

Having dyed, rinsed and dried the cloth, further string can be wound round the original and continued beyond this to cover part of the dyed area. The width of binding can vary so that the stripes of the pleated cloth and the rings of the gathered, can increase or diminish as the tone intensifies, remembering that a narrow band appears darker than a wide band of the same tone.

## Use of colour and tone

Tie and dye is not restricted to tones of one colour, but when more than one is used, their effect on one another must be realized, so that pale, clear colours should be used first and deeper, subtle ones after. In this way gradations in tone can be achieved without darkening too quickly and preventing the qualities given to the cloth by this method, from being seen. When considering the tone of the fabric in the dyebath, it must be remembered that this will dry several shades lighter.

## Results obtained from different methods of dyeing

When the string has been removed, the fabric should be washed, to shrink those areas protected from the dye, and damp ironed to remove the creases produced by the tying. The characteristic pattern given by pleating is a dark intermittent stripe formed by the knife edge of the pleat, which was not covered with string, fading and veining until the other pleated edge is reached, crossed by paler, wider stripes in the opposite direction where the cloth was bound. The gathering method produces either small rings on a darker ground, or larger ones (depending on the amount of material taken-up in tying) touching each other so that darker triangles and diamonds are formed in the background. The edge of both rings and pleats are irregular and spiky from the creasing of the fabric and flecks of a deeper tone will be seen where dye has penetrated the binding.

## Machine embroidery in relation to tie and dye

The circular patterns can be developed further by the use of fine, crisp line, given by the machine, to increase the spiky quality or give it greater definition by the use of cable stitch and cording. Patterns may be linked together by varying widths of line, or areas of white can be outlined in deeper tones of thread, in order to emphasize the more interesting shapes obtained by this method and these can be repeated in light thread on the background. Shapes which recur through the pleating process can be developed in the same way, so that the veining and texture of the dye given to the cloth, can be used to suggest various forms of patterns.

## Batik

The principle of 'resisting' the dye is again used in batik, although with wax and not string. A combination, half paraffin wax and half beeswax, is used in a melted condition, the beeswax keeping it pliable, even when hardened onto the fabric. Lawn, organdie and fine silk take the wax and dye well and since this form of 'resist' is easy to control, the preconceived design can be lightly pencilled on them and they can then be stretched with drawing pins to a frame so that the wax is not pulled off from the back of the cloth allowing the

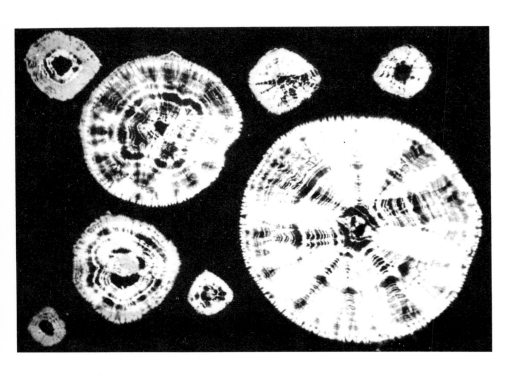

*Hull    Margaret Rackham*

dye to penetrate the fibres, as it would be if the fabric were resting against a surface. The wax, which is kept liquid in a metal bowl over heat, must not be allowed to burn as this spoils its quality; it can be allowed to smoke very gently.

## Instruments used for applying wax

Hog brushes of various sizes can be used to paint the wax onto the fabric which can be placed near a radiator or heat of some kind to prevent the wax cooling too quickly. The stiff bristles of the brush force the wax into the fibres of the fabric, are not spoiled too quickly by the heat, gives simplicity and width to the line and is able to cover large areas of fabric with wax fairly quickly. Two disadvantages of the brush are its inclination to drip and its ability to hold a relatively small quantity of wax. The first difficulty can be overcome by placing a sheet of paper over the cloth just below the area being painted.

A tjantinge, which consists of a small copper cup with a tube outlet attached to a bamboo handle, is able to keep the wax warm and apply greater quantities to the cloth. The size of the outlet can vary on different instruments, providing various widths of line, the instrument being used like a pen for continuous line until the wax is exhausted. Paper should be held beneath the bowl of the tjantinge to prevent the wax which often collects beneath it from falling onto the cloth.

## Placing of fabric in dyebath

Care should be taken if more than one waxing is contemplated, not to crumple the cloth too much in the first dyebath, since this will cause the wax to crack and allow the dye to penetrate the fibres. It is best to leave the deliberate cracking of the wax for the final dyebath when the deepest tone will 'vein' the white and pale tones most effectively. The fabric should be dried naturally after each dyebath before it is waxed any further. At the sign of bad 'cracking', areas can be rewaxed. The majority of wax can be removed by ironing between absorbent paper and the fabric can then be boiled in a solution of borax to remove the remaining wax.

## Use of embroidered line

It is not necessary to wax and dye the fabric more than once, if the colour is bright or dark, as areas of white and one colour can be augmented with different tones or colours of machine embroidery thread. If only one colour or white thread is used, the interest can be achieved by the use of different stitches and thickness of line, in contrast to the texture given to the fabric by the 'cracking' of the wax.

188

*Manchester   Julie Graham Rogers* ▶

## Painting with dyes

Painting with dyes dissolved in water allows them to spread rapidly on fine cotton and organdie, covering large areas quickly. Unless they are allowed to dry between the application of colours, they merge into further colours. See colour plate facing page 193.

*Hull   Susan Deighton*      *Bradford   Bernadette O'Donnell*

Greater control can be achieved by placing absorbent paper under fine fabrics, painting with fine brushes or working on heavier cotton, satin or sheeting.

*Manchester   Julia Jeffries*

## Dye mixed with gum arabic or printing gum

Another means of preventing the dye from spreading is by mixing a strong solution of direct dye with gum arabic; this on lawn or coarse cotton will soak into the fibres rather than creep over the surface if the consistency is correct, and will produce fairly fine lines. Dye mixed with printing gum can also be painted onto fabric with a hog brush to force it into the fibres but it is managed better in areas rather than line as its consistency is so stiff. This gives a misty, undefined edge to areas of colour which makes an interesting background for machine embroidery. All three methods of painting with dye will have to be steamed to make their colour fast and although texture can be obtained by dragging dye over the surface of the weave, it is better to have the majority of areas plain in order that the machine embroidery shall not be swamped.

## Printing with dye pressed on to paper

*Hull    Angela Jagger*

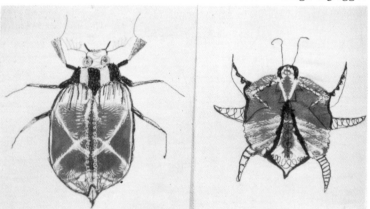

*Hull    Janet Burn*

Another method of obtaining pattern through the properties of dye is to place a little on cartridge paper, fold this so that the dye is pressed evenly and is similar in shape on either side of the crease. This can be opened and pressed down onto the fabric using card to produce an even pressure. It is sometimes possible to take a second lighter print from the paper and fine cotton should be used for this. An asymmetrical pattern can be produced by pressing dye between two separate pieces of paper and larger patterns can be built up from several of these. It is not possible to reproduce two exactly similar and this suits the individuality of machine embroidery when they are used together. Further experiments can be made with dyes of different colours on one sheet of paper or various size spots of dye which can be connected by lines of embroidery.

192

## Dye painted glass used for block printing

Prints can also be taken from dye dragged on to plate glass with a knife or stirred with a spoon or twigs and then placed face down onto fabric like a block. These can be used for texture either building up a pattern on one piece of fabric or using different textures on various fabric which can then be used for appliqué. It is also, to a rather limited degree, possible to draw on glass with dye, but it is a rather haphazard method of reproducing a design as too much dye spreads when it is under pressure and too little does not take on the fabric. If one is prepared to allow this method to produce approximate areas of colour and the embroidery to clarify this, lovely textures can be obtained which no other method of fabric printing can give.

◄ *Harvest* Strips of hessian, weaving yarns and tufting have been applied   PLATE 4
to the ground with areas of fabric stitched flat. The three dimensional aspect
of this hanging evokes the bountiful quality of harvest by its rich colour as
well as its strong tactile qualities

Dye sprayed onto hessian which has been soaked in places when the dye was
still wet to enable it to 'run'. Fabrics, cords and tufting have been added to
increase the variety of texture and enrich areas of the ground

193

Photograph of symmetrically printed fabric used in conjunction with applied fabrics and thread.

*Gay Swift*

## Direct printing from natural objects

It is possible to make direct prints from natural objects by painting the surface of shells or indented stones with dye paste and pressing them onto fine fabric placed over a pad, so that they act as wood-blocks, printing only the raised surface on the cloth. The underside of leaves can be painted so that only the veins and edges print, giving a skeleton appearance which can be developed by machine.

## Screen printing with cut paper

Printing with cut paper is a method by which the design can be built up by degrees at the printing stage. The advantages of this over applied fabric is that full use is made of the background fabric, where interesting weaves are affected by the dye and there is no fear of uneven shrinkage to which applied fabrics are subject when washed.

Absorbent paper (newsprint) is used as a stencil

placed on the cloth with a plain organdie screen placed over this. Dye paste is then pulled across the screen with a squeegee, using firm but gentle pressure in order that the dye may be forced through the screen, evenly onto the fabric not protected by the stencil.

This must be done several times in order that the dye may penetrate the fibres of the cloth evenly, but excess dye or too many strokes may cause the dye to seep under the paper and give a smudged print.

## Over-printing

It is possible to use a shape more than once as the paper sticks to the screen and this can be used for repetition or to build up a larger pattern. When a different shape is needed of the same colour, the paper can be stripped off the screen and used again, if it has not dried out, over another cut shape. The same colour over-printed on itself produces a deeper tone and different colours affect each other when they are over-printed, producing a third colour between them. As long as the whole screen has newsprint under it except where the dye is required, no unwanted dye will appear on the cloth, but if the background is to be printed, whilst the shapes are left as silhouette, then the edges of the article (if they are also intended to be white) will have to be masked with straight edges of paper.

## Enrichment of print by embroidery

The characteristic sharpness obtained by printing with cut paper is particularly suited to the crisp line produced by machine embroidery. The illustrations show how the heads were cut out with a knife, placed onto the fabric which was then masked and printed through an organdie screen with brown dye. The flowing quality given to the hair by the cut paper shapes was developed further by the embroidery line. Where only one colour is used for printing several different tones or colours of threads can be used to augment this and where several colours are printed similar coloured machine embroidery threads can be used on them in order to provide a richness which printing alone cannot give.

# 8 Uses of machine embroidery

This chapter will deal with some of the many ways in which machine embroidery can decorate articles of use. The choice of design and its placing are two of the most important factors when considering machine embroidery as a means of decoration. The shape of the article must be considered, the suitability of the fabric in which it is to be made, the placing of the motif or patterns and, finally, the form which these should take. It is possible to alter the order in which these factors are considered but they should all play an equal part in the design.

## Mats

The place mat provides a simple shape for which to design as it is two-dimensional and presents few difficulties in making up. If it is to be seen from different angles, the decoration can be placed in such a way that it reads well from any direction and can be decorated with a border, a pattern in the centre or divided into squares or triangles in which motifs are placed. A rectangular mat can have borders along two edges or can be divided into bands in which pattern is placed and since this shape is more suitable than the square for place mats, it is also possible to design it for the person in front of which it is placed, so that a single object, such as a bird, is worked in the centre of the mat and reads best from this position. Another consideration which plays an important part in the position of the design, is whether the decoration should be placed at the ends of the mat where it is visible as is shown by the decorative treatment of the knife, fork and spoon or in the centre where it is nearly always covered by the plate. The former is more sensible but the latter offers greater opportunities for decoration, since the space is not restricted but if this position is chosen, the embroidery must marry in closely with the background fabric, so that it is not raised sufficiently to make it difficult to keep the plate level. This cuts out all but the finest appliqué, straight stitching and some flat satin stitch. It is generally better to make the mats double, like an envelope so that a pad of felt can be used inside to protect the table from hot plates and can be removed when the mats are washed. If a change of tone or colour is required, it is best to print these with dyes and use machine embroidery to give fine delicate lines in contrast.

199

Colour can also be obtained from the weave of the fabric on which the mat is worked, if different colours are used in the warp and weft and also from the machine embroidery cottons if several colours are used on a plain ground. Despite all this choice, the richest effects are obtained by the use of one tone of machine embroidery cotton against a contrasting rich, bright or light coloured fabric.

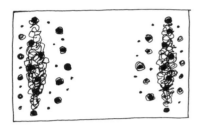

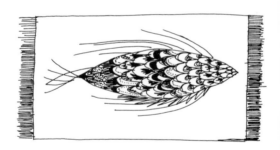

## Cloths designed to be placed under glass

Cloths for circular tables can, like the mats, be divided into sections in which the embroidery is worked, this can either stop at or extend over the edge of the table. For oval tables, decorative patterns can be worked out from an oval centre.

The circular form will help in this since there is no definite 'right way up' in its shape and a continuous border can be worked round the edge or from the centre outwards. It can also be divided into quarters, sixths and eighths, providing sections in which alternate or similar patterns or motifs can be worked. A further use of the circle is in the free placing of shapes within it to form a co-ordinated design which looks well from any direction.

*Stella Matheson*

## Table cloths

Tray cloths or table tops which are intended to be placed under glass, can be worked on rich fabrics, which would not stand laundering, and beads, sequins and gold thread can also be used, since they are to be protected. Again the design should look well from any angle, although for the tray it may be sufficient if it reads well when it is held. It may be best to use small, repetitive patterns, which form a rich background to the china and have the quality of design which will not be destroyed by an inability to see it as a whole. This is not of such importance for the table which will not always be covered with articles, so that larger, more complex shapes are possible.

Machine embroidery is particularly suited to large things such as table cloths, as the speed of working such large areas enables the designer to retain a freshness in approach even to the end, which helps to give a unity to the whole work. Many of the linens suitable for table cloths are woven in one or two colours and white, in large squares, enabling the embroiderer to use certain of these for motifs and patterns, others suggest the position of decoration by the incorporation of coarser threads or change of pattern in the weave of the fabric. In the case of plain woven fabric, the appearance can be altered by the removal or addition of a certain number of threads, so that a border is formed round the edge of the cloth or the appearance of the whole cloth may be changed. If lines of cording or satin stitch are worked every nine inches (with the grain of the fabric) in both directions, patterns can be worked in these squares all over the cloth. Decoration can also be worked in a diamond, square or circle in the centre of the cloth. If it is to fit a particular table, the decoration can be worked up to the edge of this so that none is lost where the cloth falls away. Long cloths for refectory tables can have embroidery worked down the centre with a repeat on the hem, whilst widely striped linen can have patterns and motifs worked in the stripes, facing in opposite directions from the centre of the cloth.

## Tea cosies

The tea cosy can be a difficult shape to work within, as it has one curved and one straight edge and these two opposites are often difficult to reconcile with each other. The curve can be given emphasis by allowing shapes to radiate

202

from the centre and these can be geometric in conception or based on growing form like the sunflower head and modified to a highly decorative degree. When the possibilities of the full shape have been explored, the cutting up of this into further areas can be considered. By joining two fabrics of the same type but different colours or tones, the shape of the tea cosy will be divided in half and this line can then be used to build up the design on either side. Having used the material in this way it is possible to take the idea further by working the embroidery in a counter-change pattern, by reversing the tone of the machine embroidery cotton on each side so that dark is worked on light and light on dark and areas of the opposite fabric can also be applied to increase the counter-change pattern. It is not always necessary to use thick material, organdie can be lined with felt or wool and made so that it can be taken off the padding to wash, by attaching a row of press studs round the inside, bottom edge. If cut-work is used for decoration, the fabric over which it is placed can show this up to greater advantage. Large gingham checks can also be used successfully if motifs are worked in certain checks or groups of check. It is important to choose fabrics which do not mark badly and which wash well so that the majority of rayons with a shiny finish are not very suitable. Matt fabrics also look better against china than shiny ones. Apart from the detachable pad which will need quilting if more than one fabric is used in its make-up, some manner of finishing the outer edge of the cosy must be considered and here scallops or points of the fabric might be used or a cord might be applied.

*Hull   Susan Deighton*

## Coffee pot covers

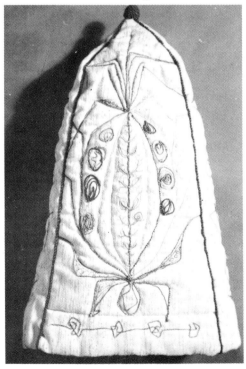

The longer shape of the coffee pot cover is rather easier to design for and suggests the use of plants, figures and buildings. They can be worked in two or four equal sections but it is often better to use narrow gussets between two wide shapes. The example illustrated, based on a plant form was first worked on the surface fabric in cable, whip and straight stitch before being quilted in cable stitch, and various tones of brown and fawn tapestry wool, star sylko and stranded cotton were used in the spool. A modification of the border pattern was used on the gussets and a hand-made cord of wool was used to cover the seams. The fabric used was a matt, cream, rayon and cotton mixture with a slight slub which has a soft handle, the lining of silk was not stiff enough alone and so had to be tacked to a backing of organdie and carded wool was used for quilting so that the whole thing might be washed.

203

## Finger plates

There is a necessity when designing embroidered finger plates, which are stretched and placed under glass, to take into consideration, not only the colour scheme of the room, but the tone and colour of the door onto which it is placed. It is serving a practical purpose in preventing finger marks, which are difficult to remove, from being left on the paint. One should be made conscious of the embroidery but it must not be so obvious in its surroundings that it 'jumps out' from the door and is instinctively avoided. The long shape is very pleasant to design for and as it is relatively small, simple plant designs and non-figurative forms will be found to work well. Fabrics with a high degree of texture should be simply embroidered and the colour kept to a subtle range, whilst simpler background fabrics will stand a richer embroidery treatment, although the use of beads will prevent the glass from fitting firmly against the embroidery, and so will allow dust to penetrate. The position of the screws must also be taken into consideration when designing, so that the embroidery is either worked round them or ceases at these points. If the door is white, the background or areas of applied fabric need to range from pale to mid tones, areas of dark tend to jump out and destroy the harmony. Lines of dark stitching may help in this case but if the door is painted a colour this can be echoed in the embroidery so that a unity is maintained between the finger plate and the door.

## Cushions

Cushions offer a variety of shapes and sizes on which decoration can be placed in many ways. It is particularly important that they should have no particular 'right way up', since they are always being moved, and while several figures used in a repetitive manner are not worrying when seen upsidedown, the appearance of one figure on its head tends to make one feel rather uncomfortable. Pattern can be worked in a border on a square cushion, but if it is taken right to the edge a certain amount is lost in the curve. Pattern can also be placed in the centre and can be based on a geometric form, since this looks the same from any side. Motifs can be placed in triangles formed by dividing the cushion from corner to corner and can either grow from the centre outwards or be placed near the edge facing inwards. The same means of dividing up the square, rectangular and circular cushion can be used as were suggested for mats, but since they are bigger, the design can be bolder and the treatment heavier. Any sort

204

of fabric which can be easily washed or cleaned is suitable for cushions, which are best made in the form of an envelope with a deep overlap of material, either at the edge like a pillow or down the centre at the back. The open end can be held down with hooks or press studs. A round bolster cushion can either have decoration in borders round it or down its length, in both cases the round ends can be decorated and it is better closed with a zip fastener. Applied fabrics can be used on all cushions as long as they are held firmly in place and the edges cannot fray, satin stitch, chain stitch and cording will all prove useful, although the latter should not be so pronounced that it becomes uncomfortable to rest against.

## Chair pads

The use of one shape which looks best only in one position is possible as long as the cushion is always seen from this angle by being taped to the seat or back of a chair. These can be shaped to the seat of the chair so that they act as a pad, their asymmetrical shape making them interesting areas for which to design. A pad can also be worked for the head and can be curved following the shape of the top of the chair. Pads can also be made for the seats of Windsor chairs, each one different but forming a link with each other by the use of fabric, method or design. Comfort must again be considered making chair pads so that the embroidery should be fairly flat, on a woollen, cotton or linen ground. Wool is very comfortable and if washed in warm soapy water and squeezed gently, rinsed several times and blotted with a towel or spin dried, will not felt and will stand up to a great deal of wear.

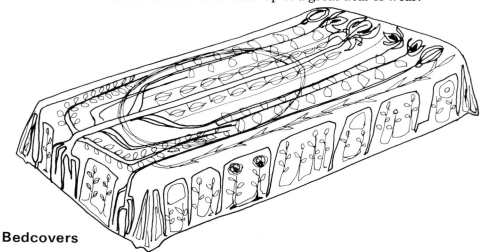

## Bedcovers

Bedspreads and divan covers, like table cloths, gain a great deal from being machine embroidered, since not only is it possible to cover large areas relatively quickly but the fabric is not handled too much and it retains its freshness. The whole of the top of the cover can be worked with a narrow border round the hem or this can be reversed so that the very rich embroidery round the edge of the bed is emphasized by the simplicity of the top. Decoration can also be taken over the pillow and round the edge of the bed, in a reduced version of this on the band holding the box-pleated or gathered material which falls at the sides. A band of decoration can be taken down the centre of the bed or a large decoration can be worked in the middle, from which small patterns radiate to the edge. Different motifs of the same or varying sizes can be embroidered all over the fabric but care should be taken if this sort of placing is used, that it would not look just as well or even better as a print.

206

## Curtains

Curtains have such a wide variety of uses that they can be embroidered in many ways on different types of cloth. Transparent curtains to be used at windows can be worked on nylon organza, ninon (fine silk plain weave) organdie, cotton and terylene curtain nets and gauze woven fabrics. These can be embroidered in fairly pale tones since the lines appear darker than they are when seen against the light. The pattern can be scattered asymmetrically over the curtain, if this looks pleasant against the window panes. If the panes are large there should be no difficulty, but if they are cut into smaller areas, they may become a distraction, unless they are taken into consideration when the embroidery is designed. This could mean that the embroidery is placed so that it falls in front of each pane and the frame holding the glass also acts as a division between flower motifs or if the design takes an architectural form, the uprights of the window can form a background to the machine embroidered lines.

Heavier curtains to keep out draughts at doors can be treated very richly since they do not have to be drawn back like window curtains. Fabrics as well as cords, beads and weaving yarns can be applied to achieve this richness in colour and texture on a heavy ground of wool or cotton repp, silk or linen. They can be cleaned if care is taken that the selection of applied fabrics are entirely of natural, rayon or synthetic fibres, like the background on which they are placed. Since this type of curtain hangs flat it is possible to treat it like a hanging or panel with shapes used together to form a composition.

## Lampshades

Lampshades require careful forethought in the design of their various shapes. The simplest is the drum, which is only slightly narrower at the top than at the bottom and which can be made in two shaped pieces. If 50 mm (2 in.) is allowed at the top and bottom and elastic is threaded through the hems, this will draw the fabric tight and enable it to be removed for washing. Those shades which taper more quickly can either be made in sections or two halves and all shades need to be lined on the inside to give a good finish. The decoration should follow the shape of the shade, either in forms within the supports which are visible when the lamp is lit, or in a continuous band pattern. Silk is the best fabric to use since the fine fibres diffuse the light evenly, cotton requires a powerful bulb to prevent the light appearing gloomy and synthetics and rayons need care as they have a low resistance to heat.

A transparent fabric with cut-work could be stretched over a silk lined shade. Cords and fringes should only be used if the appearance of the shade is improved without looking fussy.

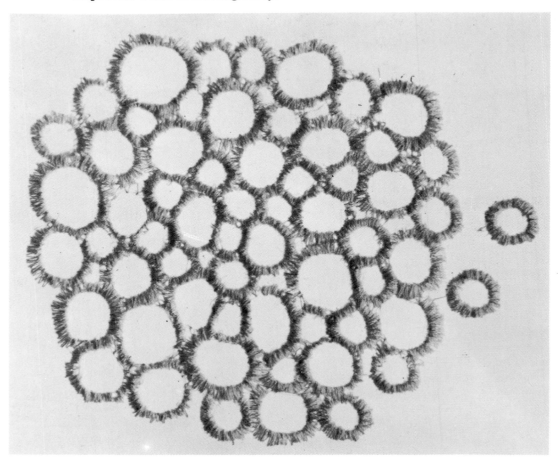

## Bags and purses

Bags of all types need a very careful choice of fabric and colour. If they are large use can be made of heavy cottons possibly in two colours with black and white machine embroidery and the use of cotton piping cords or fringe. Evening bags can be embroidered in an elaborate manner on simple fabric or very simply on rich ones and all will need very careful making-up. Cut-work circles can be used very richly if they are worked close together, leaving diamonds of fabric between the patterns. The mounting of this on to a creamy velvet or rich satin could also add further texture which would enhance the embroidery. The plush velvet used in this purse makes an interesting ground for the whipped stitching. Lurex, gold thread and embroidery cotton could all be used in cable stitching, cording and whipping to enrich a plain, tweed fabric or intricate shapes could be worked in a matt cotton thread on a rich satin with a high sheen.

*Gay Swift*

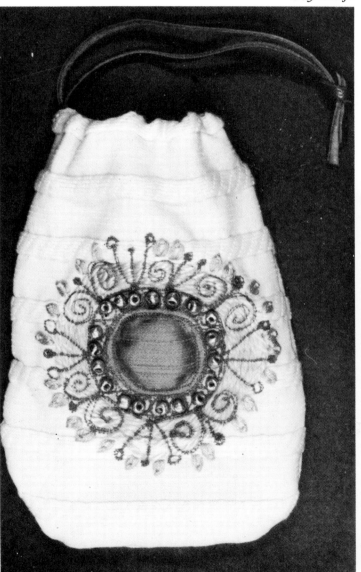

*Gay Swift*

### Boxes

Needlework and jewel boxes both offer opportunities for decoration and can be worked on, among other fabrics, silk, ribbed cotton and wool. The elastic quality of wool allows it to be stretched without sagging or loosening in any way, a useful property when it comes to making-up. The shape of such boxes are almost unlimited, so that other shapes than square, rectangular and round boxes can be made. The chosen shape should influence the design of the embroidery; geometric shapes are often best, although other simplified forms will prove decorative. A jewel box on glass fabric which has a high gloss to its surface, can have white organdie and white and fawn weaving yarns applied to off-set this with the matt quality of their texture.

### Decoration for the nursery

The nursery is an ideal setting for decoration by machine embroidery. The delicate nylons and flare-free fabrics which are easily washed, are being used for cots and suggest uses for delicate, machine embroidery on the sides and possibly the hood if the cot has one. Cot cover for older children should be designed not only to look well on the bed, but also so that the child can see it easily if he has to remain there. The cover could be built up of motifs which interest the child and either placed round the edge or spaced out in a simple layout. Table cloths might have a subject embroidered in each place worked in line and satin stitch rather than applied fabrics. Curtains either for the window, or toy cupboard, could be embroidered with a border of motifs, with smaller patterns in contrast, scattered over the rest of the curtain. Cushions and chair pads can be treated in the way already mentioned and the use of hangings rather than glazed panels, gives even greater scope for design.

The things which interest children are extremely varied, including animals, birds, insects, people, trains, buses, with people in them, cars (veteran cars can be used for design rather more easily than modern cars and even these if treated in a free way can be pleasant), boats, ships, aeroplanes and buildings. These are a few of the things which in my experience children have chosen in preference to toys, that is; dolls and teddy bears. Since most of them are realists, they need no representation of these when they actually have them to play with. They do appreciate a decorative treatment of the subjects mentioned and as a naturalistic representation of an express train roaring along in perspective is not good design, it is just as well that a simplified treatment suits them best.

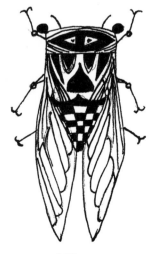

210

## Toys

Toys themselves offer opportunity for decoration, particularly the building brick, which if mounted onto strong strawboard, will be both light and strong, without causing any damage if it is thrown. The six sides give ample opportunity for ideas which will interest a child and can be worked with applied fabrics or on strong cotton printed with simple shapes, with machine embroidery to give them definition. Animals can also be embroidered but care must be taken to work the embroidery before the shape of the animal is cut out. If the seams are to be taken inside, other fabrics than felt can be used, although the crispness of shape is often lost in this method of sewing up. The legs of most animals need to be stiffened with doubled millinery wire (one length in the front and one in the back legs) so that a single, sharp end cannot hurt the child. The legs and head should first be sewn and stuffed in the same way until the back is reached when the tail can be sewn in with the last stitches.

## Ecclesiastical articles and garments

The use of machine embroidery on garments and articles is fairly recent but its influence in the 'freeing-up' of design has made itself felt to such an extent that many hand embroidered things have this freer approach. The use of materials other than brocade has become accepted for backgrounds and all sorts of different materials are now used besides the traditional silk and gold thread. The green burse shows the use of lurex fabric and threads, chiffon, felt, rayon and gold kid as well as the more traditional jap gold, purls and pearl-purls. Gold kid has been laid behind large eyelets worked on the *Irish* machine so that it glints through the holes adding to the three dimensional effect.

*Judy Barry*

Machine embroidered banner for St Luke's church, Barrow-in-Furness. ▶

*Pat Russell*

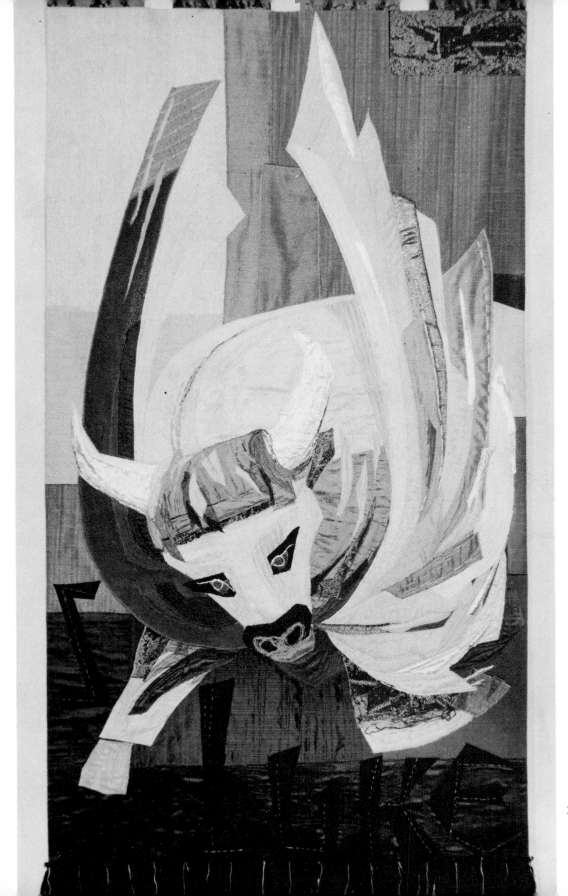

213

The detail from the Festival frontal, Alban-Neve Centre for the Deaf, Luton, shows the background enriched with layers of black net and organdie, chain stitch and straight stitch machine embroidery.

*Pat Russell and Elizabeth Ward*

## Panels and hangings

The great majority of machine embroidery done is in the field of panels and hangings, perhaps because the limitations are so few and the scope for design and the use of materials and threads so great. The variety in size is so great (from small jewel-like panels to hangings metres (yards) wide) and the content can vary so enormously, from detailed figurative elements to the exploration of the texture, colour and nature of cloth and yarns.

It is possible to obtain rich and subtle effects in the same piece of embroidery by the use not only of colour but also of the texture of matt and shiny fabrics against that of the machine line, and to stitch down only part of a piece of fabric, so that the rest of the shape curls up or stands away from the surface. Experiments should be made with a variety of fabrics in order to see their reaction to this treatment. There seems to be no reason why experiments in three dimensions should not be taken further by embroidering padded shapes which stand well away from the ground. These shapes should be worked out for their own sake and not channelled into the representation of actual objects, for the temptation then will be to pad the body of a bird, forcing the padded shape to follow this as nearly as possible with a free wing and tail added. Its greatest use would be as a decorative pattern within the shape of a subject and the way in which the fabrics react to this treatment must be allowed to dictate the sort of pattern.

It is also possible to work on different planes, so that the simple lines of the design, worked on net, can be taken further in a heavier treatment of applied fabrics on another ground and the two pieces of embroidery mounted together, so that the skeleton of the shape worked on net adds greater form to the rich interpretation of the applied embroidery beneath. If the under fabric is stretched on card and the net is mounted in a window mount with a distance of 13 mm ($\frac{1}{2}$ in.) between, it is possible to increase the realization of depth, partly through the eye being able to judge the difference in distance between the two planes and partly by the cast shadow from the embroidered lines on the net on to the fabric beneath. Further experiments can be made with semi-transparent fabrics, such as chiffon and organdie, over richer treatments of the design. These might become so complex that lighting could be used behind the two layers.

Simpler forms than the two methods just described can be used for panels: different ways of stitching on a plain ground, the use of auxiliary threads and cords for cording, the application of transparent and opaque fabrics in a flat rather than padded manner, and the use on them of stitches and patterns.

In the *Poppies* panel, there is a tremendous feeling of the movement of the poppies blowing in the wind without a realistic treatment of the flowers being used to achieve this. Instead the essence of the plant with its long stalks, seed heads and semi-transparent petals has been utilised to achieve the form from a figurative basis. The other panel is concerned with growth and harvest time and uses machine embroidery, tufting, applied fabric, yarns and loops of coloured hessian to achieve this feeling. It is concerned with the tactile qualities, with the fact that certain areas are in relief and with the alteration in the position of certain threads and fabrics.

*Audrey Tucker*

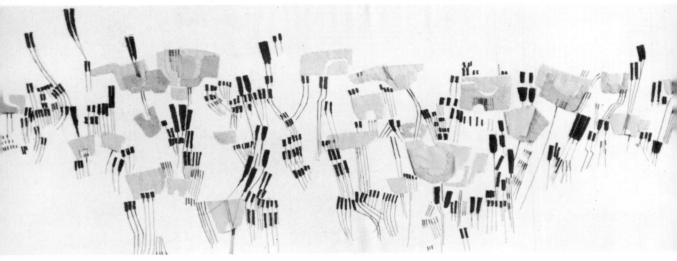

# 9  Dress embroidery

An extremely important aspect of machine embroidery is its use on dress, for which it is particularly suited, since its flexibility provides no problems when the fabric on which it is worked is draped. Delicate and bold treatments can be worked equally well on different fabrics for various purposes and since it forms an integral part of the fabric, it is easily washed. Decoration on children's clothes is dictated by the suitability of the fabric as well as the size of the garment; christening robes for instance need to be light and delicate in treatment, whether they are made in light wool for warmth or muslin.

## Christening robes

The most delicate type of embroidery is cut-work for which fine organdie is most suitable. Since the seams of this are visible, the robe should be cut either so that they do not interfere with the embroidery or so that they are incorporated into the design. If three shaped panels are used, the central panel can be placed at the front, so that the back seam will allow for an opening. If two or four panels are used, there can also be a centre as well as a back seam, which either forms a line from which the design is built or is fagotted in some decorative way. If the yoke and sleeves are embroidered, a modification of the pattern which is on the skirt, can be used. This should be reduced in size in order that the decoration shall be in correct proportion to the smaller shapes. Since the yoke is so small it is as well to shape the panels of the skirt to prevent too much fullness being gathered into it. The pieces of pattern for the robe should be placed on the fabric, tacked out and not cut until the embroidery has been worked. The advantage of this is that the tack lines can be checked to see that the embroidery has not puckered the fabric in any way and if it has, these can more easily be adjusted. If the fabric is cut with only turnings allowed, it is often difficult to frame the smaller sections of pattern for working. This method is best applied to all dress embroidery which, unless it is seamed in rare cases before working, should be embroidered on a manageable piece of cloth, with the edges of the garment tacked provisionally.

## Decoration of robes

Embroidery for christening robes need not be restricted to circles and ovals; crosses, stars, leaves, even angels can be designed to incorporate cut-work and these can be embroidered all over the panels if the design is delicate enough, in vertical borders along the seams, round the hem or in a combination of these ideas. The hem need not necessarily be straight, it can be scalloped or pointed as the design demands, either by stitching a strip of organdie to the right side of the fabric, stitching along scallops made by drawing round a coin set side by side or a triangular template, cutting the fabric close, turning the strip inside and slip stitching or sewing it down with a decorative satin stitch pattern. If the double fabric is too heavy for the hem, the edge can be stitched several times, as in cut-work, and then satin stitched before the extra fabric is clipped close to the edging. The yoke should be lined with lawn and the petticoat can also be of lawn, lightly decorated with eyelet embroidery, with the hem treated in a similar manner to the robe. When the organdie has been made-up, it should be washed and pressed several times to remove the dressing from the cloth. It is better to leave it until this moment, as this finish helps to keep the fabric firm for embroidery as well as making-up.

If the robe needs to be warmer, it can have a petticoat of light wool or flannel, or the robe itself can be made of fine wool, on which it is possible to work eyelets and small satin stitch motifs as well as cable stitched and corded lines in white star sylko or coton-à-broder, the various threads giving different textures of white against the cream of the wool.

Children's dresses and pinafores can also be embroidered and can stand a slightly heavier treatment with a bright use of colour. Cotton, linen and wool are the most useful fabrics for such clothes and terylene used in a mixture with one of these, makes a very good ground on which to embroider. In this tunic, furnishing fabric has been used and the printed pattern has been utilised as the basis for the form of the embroidery.

219

## Casual clothes

Beach clothes are exciting to embroider, since it is possible to be rather more extravagant in their decoration than with everyday clothes. The simplest shape to be adopted is the poncho, a square or rectangular garment, sewn at the shoulders and left open at the sides, which can be slipped over the head. This shape lends itself to embroidery, either in stripes or borders or with a large pattern worked centrally. This can take the form of a geometric shape or a decoratively treated subject, such as fruit, plants, fish or birds. No attempt should be made to use an object for design if it is only its aptness which appeals, for this will prevent any consideration of the shape and the treatment will tend to become an imitation of the object itself. There is nothing more unsuitable than the naturalistic representation of a yacht in full sail or a tilted bucket and spade on a child's play-suit, unless it is a scene including beach umbrellas and tables. Movement can never be interpreted satisfactorily in design as this is a static form of art, deriving its interest from the decorative quality of objects. In the same way a cunning use of line to make the bucket look real, prevents the best use being made of the shape, whilst in working a scene in a realistic manner, there is no thought to spare for the relation of its shape to the garment, apart from the lack of suitability in producing an illusion of distance on something which has to be worn. Generally non-figurative pattern is best for dress, since attention is not drawn to the embroidery but to the enrichment of the garment. Beach clothes are an exception to this and can use subject matter quite successfully if shapes are chosen which are beautiful in themselves and these are developed in a decorative, rather than a naturalistic direction. The background fabric, method of embroidery and shape of the garment should have as great an influence as the pattern on the resulting design.

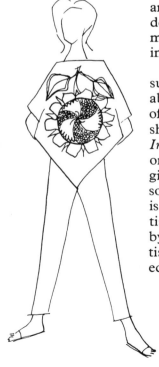

A number of fabrics can be used for beach wear: light and heavy cottons such as lawn, poplin and sailcloth for washing qualities, towelling for the absorption of moisture, and terylene mixtures for crease resistance. Blouses of soft cotton generally need little embroidery, while the heavier type of shirt in firm poplin can stand fairly rich embroidery, using the *Cornelli* or *Irish* machines to give a bold line and the domestic machine to give a corded one. For ponchos and capes, sailcloth and towelling are suitable, towelling giving an interesting texture against fabrics and applied cords and having a soft yet bulky handle. The best way to apply the decoration to the towelling is to first tack the fabric to be applied in one large piece, with the tracing on tissue paper over this, so that when the lines of the design are stitched through by machine, the applied fabric is being stitched at the same time. After the tissue paper has been torn away, the excess fabric can be cut away and the edges of the cut shapes can then be zigzagged to prevent them from fraying.

## Shorts and trousers

Beach shorts and trousers can be decorated, especially if the blouse or shirt are simple in cut. A small border on the cuff of the shorts is generally sufficient, while trews which are tight fitting round the calf and ankle, need to be slit a short way to allow the foot to emerge and this provides the obvious position for any decoration which can be taken further round the hem or up the outer seam. More elaborate lounging trousers can be embroidered all over.

## Blouses

Blouses can be richly or lightly embroidered, according to their purpose. If they are buttoned, these and the button holes can be decorated and bands can be worked on either side. If a small collar is used it is best to leave this plain to form a smooth contrast to the rest of the blouse; decoration on it will tend to make it look fussy. Embroidery is better used on a large collar to emphasize the line of the blouse or on the tie of an otherwise plain over-blouse. Mention has already been made of the use of non-figurative pattern in dress; it is generally better not to use modified forms of objects for small areas of embroidery, since in small amounts one is more conscious of texture, if a definite shape is used, attention is distracted from the garment to this. The appearance of the fabric can be altered completely by the use of embroidery all over the blouse and for certain silk day and evening blouses this can be very effective.

221

## Skirts

The skirt is perhaps the most usual garment to embroider because it offers such a choice in the position of the decoration, either on the waist band or hem or on certain panels which are an important feature of the skirt's design. In casual skirts, panels can be of different colours with the embroidery used in counter-change (light embroidery on dark fabric, dark thread of the same colour on light). This is often most successful when one colour and a neutral tone or two tones yellow and white or a pale and mid-green or a mid- and dark green. The difference in tone between the two fabrics should not be too great and the embroidery can then be worked either equally on all the panels, reversing the colour for each or more embroidery can be worked on alternate panels allowing the richness of the fabric to give the interest in the others. It is also possible to screen print the panels by cut paper method, and then embroider with a swing-needle machine areas of satin stitch which were similar to some of the printed shapes as well as fine lines which were difficult to produce by this method of printing. Fabrics can also be applied but must either be preshrunk with the skirt material or fabric of the same type as the skirt must be used so that the two shrink uniformly when washed. It is best to allow lines of decoration as well as the zigzag round the applied shape to hold it to the ground.

## Day dresses

Day dresses in cotton linen and wool all embroider well and the properties of each should be used to the full. The washing qualities of cotton and its less-fraying tendencies make it suitable for applied decoration, the ability of linen to pleat well suggests the use of embroidery beneath pleats which is visible at times, whilst the matt texture of wool acts as a foil to the sheen of the machine embroidery cotton. Decoration can be worked on a front fastening either as far as the waist or to the hem, round the neck or on the sleeves. It is also possible to embroider the whole fabric in the length before making-up, as was done in the case of the lime green woollen dress which was kept purposely simple, allowing the resulting fabric to produce the greater effect. If the dress is very simple, the one dramatic detail can be emphasized with embroidery, such as a high neck providing the right position for a rich necklet of decoration, suggested by the study of such decorations taken from tombs or seen in reproductions of mosaics. If the front of the dress is to remain plain, a band can be worked down the length of the sleeve or the whole of the sleeve can be embroidered. Other positions of embroidery will depend on the present line of which full advantage should be taken.

## Decoration of evening wear

Evening wear suggests the greatest possibilities for dress embroidery as it does not have to be so functional and it is possible to use methods without considering the necessity to wash or clean the garment. Beads, gold thread, lurex, rosettes, preconstructed flowers, sequins and cords can all be used with the machine embroidery to alter the surface of the fabric. The advantage of this over richly woven or printed fabrics, is that the decoration can be placed where it will enhance the fabric and flatter the wearer as well as accentuate the line. A cocktail dress can be embroidered in such a way that the placing of a plain jacket or blouse of the same fabric over it will turn it into a day dress or suit.

## Evening coats

Evening coats can be filmy, showing the dress beneath and will look lighter and more transparent if heavy cording and satin stitch are used in their decoration. This might be kept to the yoke so that the gathered fabric falling from it retains its bouffant quality or the skirt of the coat can be covered with decorative stars or circles, increasing in size as they reach the hem. If a sculptured shape is aimed for, a heavier fabric is better, nylon velvet (the pile of which damp presses well), heavy silk or satin. These should all be worked on a light stiff backing of organdie, so that a frame is not always necessary. When the embroidery is finished, any backing which is not held to the fabric by this, should be tacked loosely and invisibly before being seamed in with the material.

223

## Evening dresses

Evening dresses can be made in every sort of fabric, from cotton, wool, linen and silk to synthetics and rayons. Many voiles and nylons with woven stripes or gauze weaves can be enhanced with heavy embroidery on some of the stripes to emphasize the filmy effect of the rest of the dress. The use of contrasting fabrics on the same dress can also be interesting, a fine chiffon which is semi-transparent and matt against a satin, silk shantung with velvet or the use of semi-transparent and opaque fabrics applied to nylon organza.

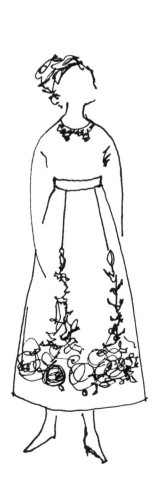

## Decoration used to emphasize the prevailing line

Since embroidery depends entirely on fashion for its position and importance on dress, it should be used to emphasize the character of the garment with regard to the prevailing line and not added after the design has been conceived in order to make the garment 'more unusual'. The raising and lowering of the waistline is one of the most noticeable changes in fashion and the emphasis of this by embroidery offers great scope for decoration. When it is raised below the bust this can be emphasized with a line of embroidery which can also be taken down the side to the waist, hip or hem, while the lowered waistline can be decorated with a band resting on the hips, which can also be taken round to the back of the garment. A line which dispenses with the waist suggests a further emphasis of this by the use of embroidery down the garment, either in a straight band or shape widening to the hem, whilst those garments which depend on a back interest either in a floating panel or pleat offer another position for embroidery.

## Complete or partial alteration of fabric by embroidery

In certain cases it is possible to alter the entire appearance of the fabric by embroidery and to give it a texture which weaving and fabric printing are unable to supply. By working out the position of the embroidery with relation to the pattern so that darts and other cutting details do not interfere too much with it, the fabric can be worked in the piece before the garment is cut. If this method tends to waste areas of embroidery, the shape (including turnings) can be tacked and the embroidery worked slightly beyond these areas to allow for a certain amount of taking-up, which the embroidery of the fabric might involve. It is possible to use the same linen for a coat as for the dress under it and by removing some of the warp and weft threads, to alter the appearance of one of them. If the drawn thread is used for the coat and the fabric is firm enough (probably a terylene mixture), the inside seams can be bound so that the dress is visible beneath it. The use of open side seams gives particular meaning, since the difference in texture of the dress and coat can be seen at this point. If the coat is to be lined with a contrasting colour and the reason for altering the fabric of one of two garments is that the difference shall be seen, the coat should be designed to show something of the dress when they are worn together. This can either be designed as a jacket or a shorter than full-length coat or the neck line of the two garments can be designed in such a way that the dress is visible above that of the coat.

The satin stitching at the edge of the drawn thread should be worked in self-colour machine embroidery thread as this will not only give a more subtle appearance than a change of colour but will add a further texture to the fabric. Where straight stitching, cording, cable and satin stitching are used, the same principle applies and tones of the fabric as well as white and black will often look richer than the use of several colours, for these tend to draw attention to the embroidery, which then becomes divorced from the garment.

225

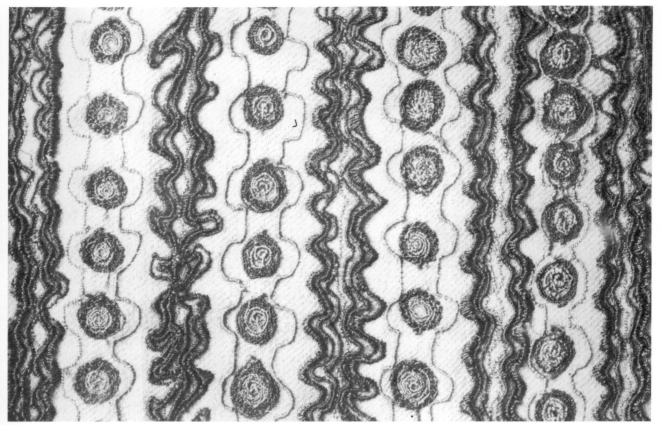

*Goldsmiths'  Judith Standeven*

A variety of different textured threads is of greater use in dress than a wide choice of colour and their possibilities should be developed before experimenting too soon with colour. Lurex used with restraint can increase the richness of dress embroidery, if it is stitched down with a zigzag stitch or used in the spool. It can be obtained in various colours, the deep ones looking best if they are stitched with black machine embroidery cotton. The advantage of gold and silver coloured lurex over most metal threads, is that it does not tarnish but its colour is not as rich and as it is so narrow, a heavy line cannot be obtained in it unless several strands are used together.

Briefly the important points to remember when designing for dress embroidery are:

Size and suitability of the design for the garment.

The relation of the design to the shape of the garment.

The use of decoration to accentuate the line.

The use of non-figurative pattern for small areas of decoration.

The importance of the colour and design of the embroidery in enriching the garment and not drawing the attention away from this to the embroidery itself.

226

# Acknowledgement

I should like to express my grateful thanks to all those who helped me with the original manuscript, a large part of which has been retained in this book, and to those who have helped me with the new version, especially Mrs Lilian Willey for her advice; Maureen Huntley for correlating the new writing with the original script; Margaret Traheren, Judy Barry, Gay Swift, Joy Clucas, Pat Russell and Audrey Tucker for the use of their work; F T Coleclough ATD, FRSA, Principal of Bradford College of Art, D S Sugden ARE, ARCA, FIBD, Principal of Hull Regional College of Art and Crafts for the use of students' work; B C C Hirst Hon ADS, ATD, Head of the Faculty of Art, Manchester Polytechnic, Anne Butler ATD, Head of the School of Embroidery, Judy Barry ATC, Lecturer in machine embroidery, and the students of this department for permission to use photographs of their work; John Thompson, Principal of Goldsmiths' College, Constance Howard ARCA, Head of the School of Textiles and Fashion, Christine Risley ATC, Lecturer in machine embroidery and their students for the use of photographs of their work; Nancy M L Lamplugh ARCA, for all her help in correcting the original manuscript on dyed and printed grounds; John E Tovey for his help and advice on woven fabrics; and the Trustees of the Victoria and Albert Museum for *Madonna and Child* page 129, the University of York for permission to include *Eclipse*, plate 3 and the Bristol Waterworks Company for *Bulb*, plate 2; also my thanks to Thelma M Nye of Batsfords who prepared the layout.

*Beverley 1973*                                                    JG

# Suppliers

**Machines**
Machines may be purchased only from authorised stockists. A list of these appears monthly in the national major sewing magazines. See also the Yellow Pages of the telephone directory

Information from
*Bernina Sewing Machines*
50–52 Great Sutton Street
London EC1

*E Pearson and Company*
82 Dickenson Road
Manchester 14    for *Cornelli*

*Husqvarna Limited*
High Lane
Stansted, Essex

*Necchi Great Britain Limited*
Titchfield House
69–85 Tabernacle Row
London EC2A 4BB

**Attachments, needles and spools**
From agents supplying machines

**Curved scissors**
Department stores
Main branches of *Boots Chemists*

**Embroidery threads and accessories including embroidery rings, hoops and frames**
*Mrs Mary Allen*
Turnditch, Derbyshire

*E J Arnold and Son Limited*
(School Suppliers)
Butterley Street
Leeds LS10 1AX

*Art Needlework Industries Limited*
7 St Michael's Mansions
Ship Street
Oxford, OX1 3DG

*The Campden Needlecraft Centre*
High Street
Chipping Campden
Gloucestershire
also gold lace

*Craftsman's Mark Limited*
Broadlands, Shortheath
Farnham, Surrey

*Dryad*, Northgates
Leicester LE1 4QR
also equipment for screen printing

*B Francis*
4 Glentworth Street
London NW1

*Fresew*
97 The Paddocks
Stevenage
Herts, SG2 9UQ

*Louis Grossé Limited*
36 Manchester Street
London W1

*Harrods Limited*
London SW1

*Thomas Hunter Limited*
56 Northumberland Street
Newcastle upon Tyne
NE1 7DS

*Mace and Nairn*
89 Crane Street
Salisbury, Wiltshire

*MacCulloch and Wallis Limited*
25–26   Dering Street
London W1R 0BH

*The Needlewoman Shop*
146–148 Regent Street
London W1R 6BA

*Nottingham Handcraft Company*
(School Suppliers)
Melton Road
West Bridgford
Nottingham

*Christine Riley*
53 Barclay Street
Stonehaven, Kincardineshire
AB3 2AR

*Royal School of Needlework*
25 Princes Gate
Kensington, SW7 1QE

*The Silver Thimble*
33 Gay Street
Bath

*J Henry Smith Limited*
Park Road, Calverton
Woodborough
nr Nottingham

*Mrs Joan L Trickett*
110 Marsden Road
Burnley, Lancashire

*Wippell Mowbray Church Furnishing Limited*
11 Tufton Street
Westminster SW1

24 King Street
Manchester

1 Cathedral Yard
Exeter

**Rug wool**
*Hugh Makay and Company
Limited*
Freemans Place
Durham City

**Vanishing muslin**
*MacCullock and Wallis
Limited*
25–26 Dering Street
London W1R 0BH

Department stores

**Leather, gold and silver
kid**
*The Light Leather Company*
16 Soho Square
London W1

**Suede and leather offcuts**
*Redpath Campbell and
Partners Limited*
Department CH13
Cheapside
Stroud, Gloucestershire

**Dyes for fabric printing,
gum arabic**
*E J Arnold and Son Limited*
(School Suppliers)
Butterley Street
Leeds LS10 1AX

*Crafts Unlimited*
21 Macklin Street
London WC2

*Dryad*, Northgates
Leicester LE1 4QR
also equipment for screen
printing

*Reeves and Sons Limited*
Lincoln Road
Enfield, Middlesex
and branches

*George Rowney and Company
Limited*
10 Percy Street
London W1
and branches

*Winsor and Newton Limited*
Wealdstone
Harrow, Middlesex
51 Rathbone Place
London W1
and branches

## USA

**Machines**
Machines may be purchased
only from authorised stockists.
A list of these appears
monthly in the major sewing
magazines. See also the
Yellow Pages of the telephone
directory

**Dyes for fabric printing**
*Arthur Brown and Brothers
Inc*
2 West 46 Street
New York NY 10036

*The Craftool Company*
1 Industrial Road
Wood-Ridge
New Jersey 07075
also equipment for batik

*Fezandie and Sperrle Inc*
103 Lafayette Street
New York

*A I Friedman Inc*
25 West 45 Street
New York NY 10036

*USA continued*
Stafford–Reeves Inc
626 Greenwich Street
New York, NY 10014

*Winsor and Newton Limited*
555 Winsor Drive
Secancus
New Jersey 07094

**Embroidery threads and
accessories**
*Appleton Brothers of London*
West Main Road
Little Compton
Rhode Island 02837

*American Crewel Studio*
Box 553 Westfield
New Jersey 07091

*American Thread Corporation*
90 Park Avenue
New York

*Bucky King Embroideries
Unlimited*
121 South Drive
Pittsburgh
Pennsylvania 15238

*The Needle's Point Studio*
1626 Macon Street
McLean
Virginia 22101

*Yarn Bazaar*
Yarncrafts Limited
3146 M Street
North West Washington DC

**Leather, gold and silver kid**
*Aerolyn Fabrics Inc*
380 Broadway
New York

229

# Index

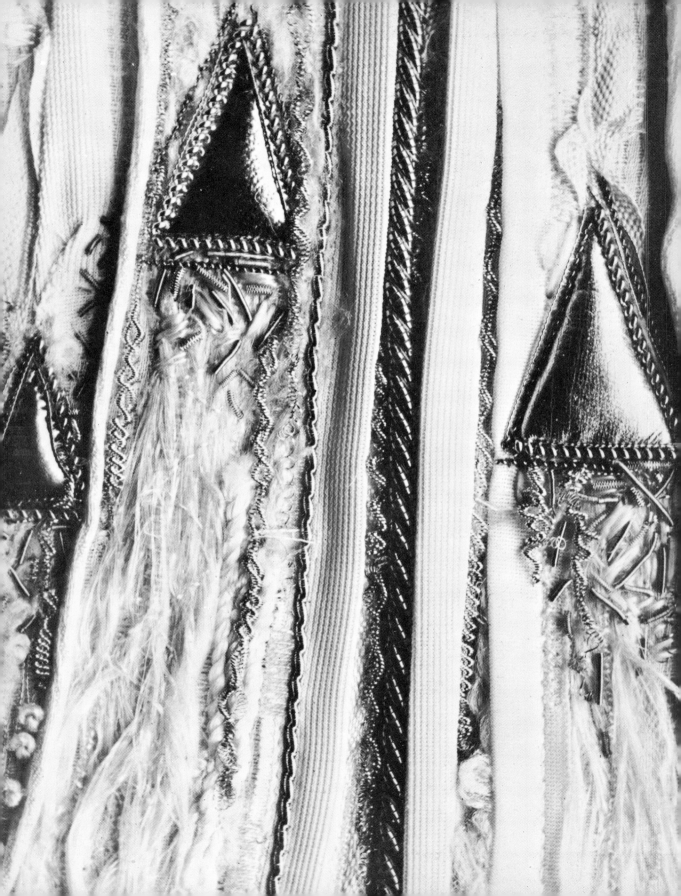